SOCIAL MEDIA MARKETING STRATEGIES

Complete Step-By-Step Guide How to Start and Grow Your Business Using Instagram, Facebook, YouTube, etc.

TABLE OF CONTENTS

Introduction

A well-established fact is that no business in this day and age can survive without marketing. Marketing has a very important impact on how you sell your products and services. The right marketing strategies can help you attain any set goals and earn more money. However, marketing is not the same as it was before and is subject to ever-changing trends. Marketing has seen a drastic change in the last decade and for the better.

The one thing that hasn't changed over the years is that you have to have a unique selling proposition. Nearly every other aspect of marketing has undergone many changes over the years. The biggest out of this is probably the impact technology has had on marketing. It is not just about setting up hoardings or TV advertisements anymore. You don't have to hire some big ad agency to market your business in order for it to be successful. Your choices are no longer limited to print or television or radio. All of these were prominent in traditional forms of marketing and are still used, but not the same way as before.

A whole new world of marketing opened up with the Internet boom and devices like smartphones and laptops becoming commonplace. It helped start a brand-new aspect of marketing; social media marketing. This book is all about social media marketing and how you can use it to market your business effectively. It is important to learn more about the various social media platforms before you venture into social media marketing, so this book will guide you through it. A notable difference between traditional forms of marketing and social media marketing is the communication channel.

Traditionally, communication was one way, i.e., from the business to its recipients. In social media marketing, communication flows both ways and is an open channel that people appreciate. As you read this book, you will learn about what social media marketing is, the different social media platforms that are prominent in the world of social media marketing, and how to successfully use them for your business.

Social media is not just for catching up with old friends anymore. Once you start using social media marketing strategies, you will realize why it is here to stay. Regardless of what the size of your business is or where in the world you are located, social media marketing is for you.

Chapter One

Social Media Marketing

S ocial media has incredible power in today's world. Nearly every person you know is active on some form of social media or the other. This has allowed social media marketing to become an eminent force in the world of marketing. It allows you to tap into social media for branding and also to bring more attention to your business and generate higher profits with more customers from across the world. You have to dive in headfirst if you want to take advantage of social media for your business. It may seem a little confusing at first, but that is what this book is for. Get rid of any assumptions or notions you may have and keep an open mind to the possibilities of social media marketing.

So, what is social media marketing? It is the process by which you can use social media to gain website traffic, generate leads, and drive sales, and much more by gaining the attention of consumers around the world. It involves the creation of content that is tailored for the social media platforms on which it is posted so that it drives higher user engagement and encourages sharing.

Every business wants more traffic on their sites or blogs, and social media marketing is a way to attain this. However, how do you use social media to generate more traffic? The most important thing is to create good content that is suitable for a particular social media platform. Every platform is different and requires a different kind of content. On some platforms, the pictures you post are of utmost importance while on another blog content is crucial. Similarly, others might require better video content or just some well-put words in a short format. For instance, you should upload high-quality photos on Instagram and well-written status on Facebook.

Every social media platform will need to be used with a slightly different strategy for effective marketing. It may seem simple to some, but it is not because of the high amount of competition. Everyone is trying their best to generate the best content and to make it go viral. This means you have to try harder and create even better content that will grab the attention of users on any particular platform. Your content has to be engaging, and people should like it enough to want to share it with others. If your content fails to engage people in this way, your social media strategy is not effective and needs to be re-thought. Context is just as important as content because people will focus more on some short content with great context than a long one with something good in the middle of it.

When you are starting out with social media marketing, it may be confusing to decide what platforms you should use. There are actually a few hundred of them on the Internet, and you can take your pick. However, we recommend that you start with the bigger platforms that have been around for longer and have a larger user database. You can always try a newer one and see if it pays off, but we recommend that you focus on something that assures better rates of success at first. This book will focus on guiding you through social media marketing on larger platforms like Facebook, Instagram, YouTube, and some more. Once you get started with applying the strategies mentioned in this book, you will soon be a Master of Social Media Marketing.

Social media marketing is ideal because it works for every type and size of business. You might have a small homegrown business, or you may be running a large company with thousands of employees. Social media marketing will work effectively for any business. In older times, traditional marketing was only accessible to big companies with a lot of funds for investing. Small businesses could not afford to pay for hoardings or advertisements in newspapers. Most forms of traditional marketing cost hundreds or thousands of dollars. However, with social media marketing, there is no such investment requirement. Social media marketing is absolutely free and hence accessible to everyone. What you need is time and some effective strategies to make it a successful marketing venture for your business. There are no hidden costs involved, and you only have to invest money when you want to use some optional features.

Social media exists in many different forms:

- Blogs

- Forums

- Social networks like Facebook

- Media sharing sites like YouTube

- Voting sites

- Bookmarking sites

- Review sites like Yelp, etc.

You may be wondering: Is social media marketing really important? Well, the answer is definitely yes. It is one of the most effective and important aspects of marketing in the world right now. Not tapping into the benefits of social media marketing will only have a negative impact on your business and make you miss out on a world of possibilities. Statistics show that there are more than 3 billion active users on the Internet right now. These numbers are definitely an indicator that social media plays an important role in marketing. The competition is fierce these days, and ignoring social media will only cause your business to be left behind while others move forward and grow.

Chapter Two

Benefits of Social Media Marketing

L et's take a more in-depth look at the benefits of social media marketing. Social media is valued in different ways from different perspectives. For someone with a business website, social media marketing can increase traffic by using strategies like SEO. However, social media does a lot more than just increasing traffic as well. Relationship building is one of the key benefits you get. It helps build trust, and this, in turn, helps to increase sales. Social media gives you the opportunity to do this. There are many reasons why social media marketing is better than traditional marketing. So, let's look at all the key benefits of social media marketing.

Improved Brand Awareness

In digital marketing, social media is probably the most cost-effective way to increase brand visibility. If you implement the right social media strategy, it will help to increase your brand's recognition significantly since it allows you to engage a much larger audience. Once you create social media profiles and engage with more users, your brand recognition slowly builds. Having people interact with the content you post will increase brand awareness and build a reputation for your business. When posts are shared, your content is given new exposure, and your brand gets introduced to a whole new network of potential customers. It is always better to have as many people become aware of your business as possible. If you just invest a few hours in a week for social media marketing, it can increase brand exposure

7

drastically. Just having a social media page can immensely benefit your brand. Using the social media profile regularly will help engage and generate a larger audience for your business.

Higher Inbound Traffic

Inbound traffic will be limited to the usual number of customers your business has if you don't market it on social media. People who are familiar with your brand will most likely be searching for keywords that your brand already ranks for. If you don't use social media marketing, it is very difficult to reach people outside of the current customer base. When you add social media to your marketing strategy, every social media profile will give you access to a new customer base. Every post on social media gives you an opportunity to acquire new customers. People on social media come from different places, backgrounds, and have different behaviors. They also have different needs and ways of thinking. When you syndicate your content on different platforms, it allows different people to reach your business in an organic way. Social media marketing allows your business to attain potential consumers from all over the world.

Improved Search Engine Rankings

When you post on any social media site, you will see increased traffic to your website. However, it is not as simple as that if you want to see any significant success. For higher traffic and page rankings, it is important to utilize search engine optimization. Social does not increase search engine rankings directly. However, it does help to improve search engine rankings quite significantly within a year of social media marketing for most businesses. If you can be in top positions for specific keywords related to your business, it can revolutionize the amount of traffic that your business gets. A common fact is that most people use Google to search for any information. Another fact is that they rarely go beyond the search results that are displayed on the first page. Search engine optimization for your brand should be strategized in a way that puts your website on the first page of search results. If it doesn't, then you need to change your strategy. Create high-quality content while integrating the targeted keywords in order to increase ranking. Your social media profile will be much more credible if you have content like blogs or employee photos or business information. Posting quality content on various social media will help you build a community that will constantly be liking or sharing it with others. This will make your brand more visible to influencers who will promote your brand by writing about it or providing links.

Higher Conversion Rates

An increase in visibility will provide your business with more opportunities to convert customers. Any image, blog post, or video can help increase traffic and lead viewers to the business website. Your business gets the opportunity to create a positive impression by using social media marketing. Brands that interact by commenting, sharing content, or posting statuses, tend to have a better brand personality. People are attracted to the humanization factor and become more willing to do business with such brands. Studies showed that marketers observed increased sales when they took the time to interact and create a relationship with their consumers. Creating a good impression on visitors will make it more likely that they think of coming back to your business when they need a product or service that you offer. Compared to outbound marketing, social media can increase lead-to-close rates a lot more. Brands that are interactive online will have more followers and develop more trustworthiness and credibility. Use social media to convert as many potential consumers as possible by being interacting with as many people as possible.

Higher Customer Satisfaction

Social media is basically a platform for communication and networking. If you want to humanize your company, you have to use social media to create a voice for it. Customers are much more satisfied when they receive personalized replies to their comments or messages as compared to automated messages. When you acknowledge every comment made by visitors, it shows that you pay attention and are aiming to provide a good experience for your customers. Interacting with customers on social media accounts will help you demonstrate compassion for all customers in a public way. Use interpersonal dialogue to address any complaint or question any person might have. Being dedicated to customer satisfaction will help you retain your current customer base for longer and build a new one soon as well.

Improved Brand Loyalty

Most businesses aim to develop a large and loyal customer base. It is important for you to engage and bond with consumers to assure customer satisfaction and increase brand loyalty. It is not just about promotional campaigns. These social media platforms are seen as a channel of communication between businesses and consumers. Compared to others, millennials have shown the most brand loyalty. This is why it is important for all businesses to work on their social media marketing and gain the attention of consumers and influencers.

Higher Brand Authority

For more brand authority, brand loyalty and customer satisfaction play a big role. However, communication is what it all comes down to.

Your brand appears more credible to people when they see your post on social media and reply to customers about any query or complaint they have. Regular interaction demonstrates dedication to customer satisfaction, and these satisfied customers are more than happy to spread a positive word about your business. Most people use social media to express an opinion on any product or service they liked or hated. Having people post positive reviews about your brand on social media will show consumers your brand value and increase authority. Even obtaining a few satisfied customers and having them express their positive experiences to others will help advertise your brand. The best advertising is satisfied customers recommending your brand to other people.

Costs are Minimal or Free

If you look at your entire marketing budget, you will see that social media marketing is the most cost-effective. Nearly all social media platforms allow you to sign up and create profiles for free. They do offer paid promotions, but even those are optional and at minimal cost compared to any other marketing tactic. The cost-effectiveness of social media marketing will allow you to see greater returns on your investment and also help you keep more money aside for other business expenditures. Utilize all the free options on social media before you start using paid promotions. Once you start using paid advertising, start small and see what works. You can slowly increase your budget as you fine-tune your social media strategy. A little time and money go a long way in increasing conversion rates. The best part is that the money you invest will show much greater returns if you carry out your strategy well.

More Marketplace Insight

Social media gives you the advantage of more marketplace insight. You can communicate directly with consumers through social media, and this allows you to learn their wants or needs. When you monitor consumer profiles, you get to learn a lot more about their interests, likes, and dislikes than you ever could before. If your business doesn't have a social media presence, you lose out on the opportunity to get such personal insight on consumer needs. Social media can be used as a research tool that helps you understand your industry more. Gaining a large number of followers will help you utilize analyzing tools to get more information. You will also be able to segment the content syndication lists on the basis of the topic and learn what kind of content will generate more impressions. Such tools allow you to measure conversions on the basis of posts from various social media platforms and help you find a way to generate more revenue.

Enable Conversation

Traffic is just that, isn't it? It is traffic. This is not true. What you should care about is how you can drive conversation through traffic. Let us look at some ways in which you can drive traffic on social media:

Always Add Calls to Action

When you add calls to action to your posts, it will motivate your customers to do something. They will always want to purchase your product. If you look at the description for this book, you will see that you are asked to purchase the book if you want to improve your visibility on social media platforms. It is also a good idea for you to design the messages you post on your pages in a way that will appeal to the customer. When you do this, you can ensure that they purchase your product. You can always place these advertisements anywhere on your social media page. Direct your customers to your website when they click on the advertisement. The trick is always to ensure that your customers are engaged and want to purchase your product. Make sure that the entire process is engaging so that the customer does not back out from purchasing the product.

Contests

Businesses never want to host contests. They also do not want to give free stuff away, but these do help improve your business. People will be compelled to purchase your products if you have given them some free stuff in the past. If you check Instagram, there is at least one business every day that gives free stuff away. Businesses often use their social media pages to post images and content that will encourage their customers to spread the word about their products. Instagram has many such posts and stories where businesses encourage users to tag their friends for free stuff. All you need to do to win the stuff is:

1. Follow their page.

2. Repost the image as your story or post.

3. Tag your friends.

4. Follow the original poster.

When you use such techniques, you can ensure that your company's following increases.

Advertisements

Remember that people on social media are not there to buy stuff. They only use social media so they can stay in touch with their friends, follow their interests, or read organic content, which means that they hate looking at advertisements. The challenge here is to grab their attention and encourage them to purchase your product. You need to do this without leaving a bad impression on them. The advantage of using social media is that you can place your advertisements directly on the platform. The audience will not feel like you tricked them. Twitter and Facebook will allow you to post advertisements on the timeline of your target market. These ads will encourage your customers to your website.

Leadership

To become a leader and expert in your industry, you should use social media to post insightful, well-written content. Online networking tools help you work on this. Build your presence online by using social media platforms in the best way possible. Communication is very important, so try and connect more with your audience. Communication and content sharing promote your brand's authority. Aligning your social media campaign with any other marketing efforts will highlight your skills and grab the attention of more users. Connecting directly with consumers through social media helps to create a strong relationship with them that they value and then regard you as an influencer.

You can clearly see how advantageous social media marketing can be for your business by now. So, if you haven't already created the appropriate social media profiles for your business, it is time to get started. This book will help you tackle social media marketing strategies using various different platforms. Start posting some engaging content and watch as your followers increase. As long as you keep up with your social media campaign, you will watch your followers grow, and conversion rates increase. The sooner you get started with social media marketing, the faster your business will grow.

Chapter Three

How to Create a Social Media Strategy for Your Business

The key to doing well in social media marketing is a good strategy. If you don't have a strategy, you will just be posting on various platforms for the sake of posting. When you don't have any identified goals or don't know who your audience is, you won't be able to achieve anything from social media. If you want to be a successful social media marketer or grow your brand through it, an excellent social media strategy is essential. We have put together simple guidelines to help any beginner create a social media marketing strategy with ease.

Firstly, you have to understand that a plan and a strategy are different despite having many crossovers. Your strategy is where you are headed, but your plan is about how you'll get there.

To create a social media strategy, you need to ask yourself the following questions:

- Why do you want to use social media in the first place?

- What audience are you targeting?

- What content do you plan to share?

- Where are you going to share your content?

- When are you going to be sharing content on social media?

The interesting thing about social media strategies is that you can have a different strategy for each social media channel that you choose to use. For instance, your Facebook social media marketing strategy might be different from the strategy you have for marketing on Twitter. All of these strategies together will comprise of your overall social media marketing strategy for your business.

Here we will focus on the overall social media marketing strategy for your brand:

Why Do You Want to Use Social Media in the First Place?

The first question to consider is why you want to be on social media platforms. This means you have to think of the goals you want to attain through social media. Maybe you want to use social media to promote products or services. You may want to use it to drive more traffic to the main business website. You may just want to use it to connect with customers.

For most businesses, there are a few common goals that are to be attained with the help of social media marketing:

- To increase brand awareness

- To drive more traffic to the business website

- To generate more leads

- To increase revenue

- To increase engagement

17

- To provide customer service

- To build a community for your business/brand

- To learn what the general consensus is about your brand

- To increase publicity about the brand

You might have one or more of these goals for your business. However, it is better to focus on a few at a time and not have too many goals at once. You can tackle more if you have a larger team and can distribute responsibilities to different people to tackle each goal.

What Audience Are you Targeting?

After you figure out what your social media goals are, you have to focus on determining a target audience for your campaign. Every business has to narrow down on its target audience, or they won't know how to appeal to them in the right way. Zeroing in on a target audience will also help you figure out the rest of your social media strategy. So, if you are a children's clothing brand, you have to focus on women who have children or are about to. This is just an example to explain how you have to determine your target audience. If you are a travel company, you can focus on people who are very interested in traveling often.

The following pointers will help you build personas for your audience:

- Who are these people in terms of gender, age, jobs, location, etc.?

- What can you provide for these people?

- What social media platforms do these people usually use?

- What time of day are these people usually active on social media?

- What are they looking for when they search for content?

- What form of content do they prefer in terms of videos, blog posts, etc.?

It won't be very difficult to determine who your target audience is. If you have been running a business for a while, you get an idea about the general buyer persona. Just write these things down and focus on this as your target audience.

What Content do you Plan to Share?

Once you decide on your audience, you may start thinking about the kind of content you want to share. Here you should focus more on a theme rather than types of content. For instance, as a travel company, you may want to focus on sharing high-quality pictures of people in exotic locations. You don't need to focus on a single theme, but having at least a couple of different themes for your page allows your audience to know what to expect when they follow you on social media. Different themes will also help you have the option of more variety to share. Take a look at the persona you determined earlier and think of how you can help them or appeal to them. For instance, if your brand sells fitness equipment and apparel, you can upload images and videos of different exercises while using those products. This will give your customers a better idea about your products and also make them more willing to purchase them. As we said before, finding your target audience plays a big role in creating a social media strategy.

Where are you Going to Share the Content?

The next step is determining the social media platforms that you intend to use. Where do you want your brand to have a presence? Remember that you don't need to create a profile on every single social media platform out there in a bid to reach more customers. When you determine your target audience, find out which platforms they use more as well. If you are a few platforms instead of on too many, you can focus on doing better on those. You will also have more time to create better content for those platforms. Use analytical data to figure out the platforms that your audience tends to use more often. Different people prefer different platforms, at least for different purposes. In general, the older generation prefers a platform like Facebook to connect while young adults or teenagers are more active on Instagram these days. Also, figure out what type of content you can create better. Then choose the platforms that are better suited for that kind of content. For example, if you can create great video content, you should create a presence on YouTube for your brand. It is one of the most widely used video-sharing websites at present and has millions of users from around the world. However, you don't need to worry about just providing a single type of content because most other social media platforms allow users to post different kinds of content on their channel. You should also consider using niche platforms that may be smaller compared to others. It is easier to target customers on such platforms because they are already a separately created group with a well-defined interest.

When are you Going to be Sharing Content on Social Media?

The final step is to figure out when you should be sharing content on any of these social media platforms. You should do research on the best time to post on any particular platform for a certain buyer persona, but this is not something to obsess over. You can figure out the right time to post by yourself if you take a step back and look at the performance of your own campaign. Just pay attention to the behavior of your target audience and post at a time of day that those people tend to be more active. There is no point posting at a time that your audience won't view the post, and if the time difference is too much, it may not even appear at the top of their feed when they use social media again. For instance, if your target audience is the working class, you should post at a time when they are likely to be home and resting, not during their working hours.

Once you have carried out the above-mentioned steps, you just have to figure out how to execute this social media marketing strategy for your business. This is when you have to create a plan and head towards your goals with actions. Focus on the big picture when you are developing a strategy and plan. Don't singularly focus on daily tasks and forget about what you want in the long run. A good strategy will take you far in the world of social media.

Chapter Four

Instagram Marketing 101

Instagram is probably one of the most popular social media platforms in the last decade. It has a simple user interface and appeals to people of all demographics. One of the reasons is that it is visuals based, and everyone loves sharing and looking at pictures. At first, it was just about sharing pictures with people, but now Instagram is a hub for a lot of activity. The app itself makes it very easy for people to use filters or tools to make their pictures more beautiful. Everyone is attracted to such beautiful images on their feed, and most Instagram users are guilty of spending hours on their phone just scrolling through pictures. It is also a fact that people love getting "likes" on any pictures they share on their Instagram account, and this makes it addictive for them. Instagram currently has more than a billion accounts on it, and users are active on this platform on a daily basis. Statistics also say that every user tends to follow at least a single business account even if they generally follow people they are familiar with. This makes it a great opportunity for businesses to use Instagram to connect with more users. You probably know that Instagram has great potential for your social media marketing campaign, but you may not have figured out how to go about it yet. This is where this section of the book comes to you. You will learn how to define goals for an Instagram marketing campaign and also how to target the right audience on this platform. You will also learn about the importance of having a budget for the campaign and how you can establish yourself on Instagram. To establish a well-defined marketing strategy for Instagram, you just have to follow the simple guidelines given here.

Define Goals for Your Instagram Marketing Campaign

You may or may not already have an Instagram account for your business. If you don't, it is time to create one. If you do, you need to start focusing on why you are on Instagram in the first place. Think of the goals you have for this account. Do you want to raise brand awareness? Are you looking for more leads? Do you want to use the account to convert warm leads that you already have? Do you want to connect with customers more? Any or more of these could be part of your goals for using Instagram. The important thing is to identify what your goals are. Having a clearly defined goal will set the path for the rest of your actions. You will be able to focus on your goal and work effectively. For instance, if you want to raise brand awareness and have a big budget, you will be focused on running ads while targeting your defined audience. If you want to connect better with customers, you will be focused on interacting with them via comments and running contests to build loyalty.

Define Your Instagram Audience

Once you have set a goal for your Instagram marketing campaign, you need to work on defining the target audience for this. You won't see results if you create generalized content for everyone. The Facebook Ad Manager is similar to how you will be working on Instagram as well. Ads Manager helps you customize who you want as your audience for any ad. You can select everything from a range of age and which locations these people should be from. You should also check what their interests are and target them depending on their behavior. You can choose from people who may have previously interacted with your brand as well. When you refine the audience for your ads on Instagram, it allows the ad to work more effectively and results in real conversions. Your ads should always be reaching the right people and not just be sent out to a large audience.

Determine a Budget for Instagram Marketing

The next step is to determine a budget for marketing on Instagram. Instagram marketing does not require a large budget. This allows small businesses to utilize this feature well as well. Your campaign will be especially effective if you manage to narrow down on a target audience. Refining your audience will help any Instagram ads reach the right people and thus work in favor of your brand.

So how much money should you be spending on Instagram? This will depend on the size of your business, how much money you have for marketing, and also on the goals you have for Instagram. You have to decide on a daily budget or on a lifetime budget. If you fix a daily budget, you will ensure than only a fixed amount of money is spent on your ads in a single day. If you fix a lifetime budget, you will be deciding the total amount you want to spend on that campaign in its overall duration. This money will be divided by Instagram equally over that time while running the ads. For people with a smaller budget, it makes sense to work with a daily budget. This will allow you time to check if you are actually getting your money worth. Analyze the results from the ad running on that daily budget. There is no specific guideline for how much anyone should spend on the daily budget, but you will be able to figure it out yourself as you work on it. Trial and error will help you find the sweet spot for your daily budget.

You have to determine the optimization of ad delivery as well. This is related to the business goal you set at the beginning of your Instagram marketing campaign. You need to decide how to optimize ad delivery. For instance, if you want to get more visitors on your website, you should optimize the links clicked. If you want to increase brand awareness, you should optimize for how many impressions a post or ad gets.

It is also important to keep in mind that you may want to modify your budget at times. There might be particular days when you want to increase the budget because business tends to do better on those days. Ad scheduling helps a lot in such matters. You will be able to create a schedule and run ads at any specific time and day.

Establish a Brand Presence with Consistency

The technical aspects of your Instagram marketing strategy have been covered mostly. However, you should also focus on being consistent with the brand image on Instagram. The following tips are helpful in creating a consistently good Instagram feed that your audience will appreciate:

Light and Background

Lighting and background on images should be consistent. When someone opens an Instagram account, they take a look at the overall aesthetic of that account. Consistency makes it look more professional. Visual consistency has its own appeal. For instance, if you upload food posts, try to keep the background consistent even when the food is different. You could use a white plate for every dish you take pictures of. If you want a rustic look for your overall account, use elements like wood that will add to that feeling. If you prefer taking pictures with natural light, then take all your pictures under natural light. Most pictures look better with a light background, but it should not be harsh light either. You can take a look at some popular Instagram accounts and check their theme. Figure out a theme that would work best for your brand and stick to it as well. You can take inspiration from others but establish consistency with your brand.

Filter Consistency

Use the same filter for all pictures. The filters on Instagram make it very easy to edit pictures before uploading. This point is cohesive with the previous tip. Using the same filter will give your account a better look at first glance, and we all know that first impressions are important. If you keep using different filters, your feed will look irregular and unattractive. You don't necessarily have to use a readymade filter either; you can use the various editing tools included in the app. Just give all your images a similar look. If you like more saturation, then add it to all your images. If you like brighter pictures, then increase the brightness consistently on all pictures. If your image edits are consistent, it makes every picture look better on your feed.

Consistent Hashtags

Use the same hashtags on all posts and only ones that are relevant. Don't add random hashtags that are popular but unrelated to your images. Do some research and find popular hashtags that are related to your brand and images. Keep a check on the performance of these hashtags and keep a list to use for all your pictures. You can also create unique hashtags for your brand. Allow users to share images using those hashtags when they use products from your brand. Consistent hashtag use will also make your Instagram marketing strategy simpler to carry out.

Consistency in Posting Schedule

Establish consistency in your posting schedule. Create a schedule for posting on Instagram. It helps your audience to know what to expect from your brand, and they remain interested. Don't post consistently for a week and then go off-grid for another week. If your account is suddenly inactive, users may even want to unfollow you. Instagram helps you remain consistent in your activity, as well. Use the Ads Manager to schedule posts on your account. It will help you keep on track with your marketing strategy and plan. There are various external apps or tools that help you with social media management, as well.

Brand Conscious

Copy and content should always be "On Brand." Your brand needs to have a voice that is evident in all your posts. Establishing a brand voice plays a big role in social media marketing. The copy on any of your ads or posts should keep the brand voice in mind. Always keep the core audience in mind when you create copy for your ads or posts. The copy should also be relevant to the image and provide context to it. Customers will appreciate consistent and relevant posts.

Once you nail the marketing strategy for Instagram and work on it consistently, you will be able to help your business grow. Instagram analytics will help you monitor the performance of your efforts and help you stay on track as well.

Instagram Marketing Tips

The following tips have been put together after studying the marketing tactics of other brands that have successfully used Instagram for building their brand. You can utilize these and grow your brand on Instagram too.

Create an Actionable Instagram Hashtag

Create an actionable Instagram hashtag and build a community around it. This strategy is actually useful because you can leverage that same hashtag across other platforms as well. It will help engage your audience more than a random irrelevant hashtag ever will. You can start a movement around your brand if you really work on this kind of campaign. Nike is one of the best examples of this type of marketing strategy. They encourage people to take real actions and leverage their hashtag campaigns. There are a lot of hashtags that have gone viral due to such successful marketing efforts and made a real difference.

Find a Good Cause

Find a good cause that is in line with the values of your brand and partner with them. If you do your research, you will see that some brands take a unique approach in creating their posts. They promote and share their partnerships with followers. You can form a partnership with some small business that aligns with your brand's values. It will be a relationship that supports the growth of your business as well as theirs. Being able to align your values with those of your customers will work in your favor. You can share posts with captions depicting a story that your viewers will relate to. Since the caption limit is not like that on Twitter, you have free reign to express yourself.

Understand How Your Followers Think

Keep the mindset of your followers in mind. Your posts need to relate to the mindset of the target audience, even while being relevant to the brand. The buyer personas you have established will help you understand how your target customers think. So, figure out why these people use Instagram in the first place. Are they just using it to pass the time? Do they want to keep up with what their friends or family are doing? Are they looking for solutions to something? When you post something, it has to be content that your target customers are interested in. However, it also has to be something related to your brand and should help promote your business. Your followers may be interested in interior designs, but it won't make sense just to post a picture of a pretty home if your business involves financial consultancy. In this case, your caption comes in handy because you can let them know that your financial advisor will help them buy the home of their dreams. This is the kind of tactic you have to use to keep your followers interested.

Avoid Posting too Frequently

If you are a beginner on Instagram, it is important to know that you shouldn't be posting all the time even though you can. A lot of people have a stagnant account and suddenly start posting a hundred pictures when they finally go on vacation. If you spam someone's feed at once, it makes them want to unfollow you. You may want to share a few pictures at once, but this is where you can make use of the album feature that Instagram released a while ago. This allows you to post pictures in a slideshow format on the same post. However, it is better to stick to one or two posts in a day. Being regular on Instagram is important, but don't be over-enthusiastic and post too much.

Use Other Platforms to Promote your Instagram

You will probably have profiles on other social media or have your own website. Use these to encourage people to follow your Instagram account. Add an Instagram icon on your other platforms or emails to help people find your account. The first time you set up the account, the easiest way to get followers is to connect with Facebook friends who are also on Instagram. Then get your marketing campaign running to attract new followers. When you or any employees send out business emails, they should add a link to your Instagram account to it as well. There are so many ways in which you can get people on Instagram.

Figure Out How to Put Your Brand Across in an Appealing Way
When you think of Instagram, you assume that the pictures have to be of attractive things. Most people like seeing pictures of beautiful places, food, clothes or even people. But your business may be related to something that is not actually aesthetic in the general sense. This makes many businesses reluctant to use Instagram because they don't know what to take pictures of. However, you can still find something beautiful in your business to share with people. You just have to figure out what. Even if your products are not exactly aesthetic, you can still share nice pictures of the people at work or of any events you hold. This gives your audience a way to connect more with your brand. Encourage your employees to do the same and spread a positive message about the environment at work. Adding such personal touches makes your brand more appealing to the public.

Utilize the Tools That Instagram Offers

Instagram is constantly trying to make their app better for users. There are many tools available for you built into the app. You can track performance, edit pictures, etc. You can try using any of the following tips mentioned below to optimize your brands account on Instagram:

1. Get familiar with the filters, editing tools, and effects on Instagram. You can use any of these tools to edit your images and post the most visually appealing content on your account. While there are filters that are already modified for use, you can manually edit pictures using the editing tools on the app. There are options to manipulate the saturation, brightness, exposure, sharpness, etc. You can adjust the focus, tilt, etc. on your images as well. If you have a creative team for such work, you can ask them to get familiar with these tools while creating posts. If not, these features are easy for every single person to use as well. You don't have to be an expert in photo editing to use the editing tools on Instagram. The ready-to-use filters on Instagram are easy to use and can help you maintain a consistent feed.

2. Utilize the business tools that are introduced specifically for business accounts. The Instagram analytics tool is especially useful to monitor the performance of the account over time. You will be able to check on metrics such as profile views, saves, email clicks, impressions, etc. This tool is free for use, and you can use it even if you aren't paying for Instagram advertising. You can also get insights into details like the age range, gender breakdown, locations, etc. of your followers. You can see some basic information right under the post but can use the analytics tool to get more in-depth information.

3. Be Insta-smart. The Instagram platform is ever-growing, and you need to keep updated with it. Since Instagram makes money from the advertising business, they try to make improvements in their features to accommodate their needs as well. Over the years, Instagram has already been doing a lot to help support businesses

through its platforms. If you stay informed and active on Instagram, you will be able to use it to grow your brand sooner.

Take Inspiration from Other Accounts

A lot of brands from around the world have been using Instagram for their business quite successfully. Our advice is to take the time to research these accounts and understand how you can make your account work better as well. You can find incredible accounts on Instagram that are carrying out social media marketing campaigns in the best way possible. Take inspiration from these accounts; try to copy their strategy while giving it a certain unique element. You can mimic the strategy but don't mimic the content or copy at the cost of losing brand integrity. Learn from them while creating something unique for your brand.

Interact More to Increase Followers

While your content is very important, you also have to interact with the people who follow your account or like and comment on your pictures. You should also follow other accounts and interact with them on their posts. People will appreciate engagement on their posts just like you would want it on yours. You can encourage people to use a unique hashtag created by your brand, and when they do, make sure to like and comment on their posts. You can also repost some of the better content on your feed.

Use Instagram Stories

Use the Instagram Stories feature and show followers the inside story. You need to think a lot before posting content on your feed. However, posting on Stories is another matter. You can keep it raw and friendly for your followers. Show them how things run behind the scenes. Also, let them know of any new launches or events that may be happening. You can leverage this feature to connect personally to your followers.

All of these tips should help you get a good head start on marketing on Instagram. So, start clicking and begin posting on this great platform as soon as you can.

Chapter Five

YouTube Marketing 101

YouTube is a platform with a very high traffic rate, and the number of viewers constantly using the site is also quite high. The site boasts more than 2 billion users active on it, and every minute, nearly 300 hours of content is being uploaded on it. Video marketing is an obvious trend that is only growing every minute. Regardless of whether your business is online or offline, YouTube marketing can make a huge difference for you. YouTube is a very influential platform in terms of social media marketing. To be successful in YouTube marketing, you have to get as many followers for your channel and as many views on your videos as possible.

Benefits of YouTube Marketing

Large Audience
There are about 2 billion users on YouTube across the world. It is accessible nearly everywhere and can be accessed on many different devices. It is currently being used in more than 70 countries and in nearly that many languages. As a marketer, your job will be to capture the attention of as many of these people as possible and to grow the audience for your business. YouTube allows you to gain global exposure and that much more potential customers.

Greater Visibility

Since Google owns YouTube, it provides you with an advantage in terms of search results. Every time you search for something on Google, you will usually see some related YouTube videos among the first few results. You can use this marketing technique to get a lot more visibility. Having the domain name and the name of the YouTube channel similar will help improve search results for your website. Embed your YouTube videos on your official business website as well as on other platforms to increase the ranking of your videos. Also, add the right keywords in the description of the videos to increase visibility. Greater visibility is essential for an effective YouTube marketing strategy.

Expertise

Many brands and businesses use YouTube to help them increase their authority in a specific field of expertise. They can do this simply by making YouTube videos that are relative. It helps to increase credibility and also makes the audience trust the brand or business.

Repurpose Content

You can use the content from your website or blog to make videos and post them on YouTube. The content can be made into video series, presentations, or animations as you want.

Engaging

It is much easier to connect with an audience through videos. They provide a more personal touch to content compared to many other types of marketing. Your target audience will be able to comment, like, dislike, share your videos, and engage more with you.

It's Free

Most forms of marketing can be costly, but using social media platforms like YouTube is absolutely free. You can upload as much as you want and obtain benefits without spending anything at all.

Getting Started with YouTube Marketing

It is important to understand how YouTube marketing is different from other social media channels and how you can get started with it. This chapter will help you learn how to set up a great channel, optimize and edit videos on it, and how to advertise and monetize on YouTube as well. You may already have a YouTube channel, or you may be a beginner who wants to set up one. Nonetheless, you need to go over the essential points in this section of the book.

Demographics

YouTube has a very diverse and large audience with millions of active users. According to statistics, around 11% of the users on YouTube are between 18-24 years old. 23% of its users are between 25-34 years old, and 26% of users are between 35-44 years old. Users between the age of 45 and 54 years old are 16%, while those above 50 years are 11% of the user demographic. The rest of the 14% is not determined yet. The overall summary that you have to understand is that out of every ten people that visit YouTube, 8 are between 18-49 years. Because of the increased use of smartphones, the number of YouTube users has increased even more.

To succeed in YouTube marketing, you have to approach it differently when compared to other social media campaigns. Most of the other platforms mentioned in this book are essentially used for creating content and sharing it to create awareness and increase engagement.

To put it shortly, they are for socializing. However, most users don't use YouTube for socializing. YouTube videos are mostly like blog posts, and thus YouTube marketing is better fitted towards niche-specific content marketing. The comments on these videos will be similar to comments on blogs. Users might view the videos, but they may or may not choose to engage my commenting. This is why you have to keep this in mind and focus on content marketing.

When a user wants to search your YouTube videos, they have to be specific in their search. Otherwise, they might also stumble across it when they search for similar videos. Users on other platforms can find you through ads or through some friend's engagement on your content. YouTube is more of personal experience and not so much of a social one. People don't usually tag each other here. When a user opens YouTube, they do so with the intent of watching something specific most of the time. On platforms like Instagram, users tend to scroll through without any specific purpose idly. So, when you create content for YouTube, it has to be different from the kind of content you post on social media like Instagram.

Updates

The YouTube site has undergone some changes that you need to keep in mind, as well. One of the updates prevents you from creating annotations, and instead, an "End Screens" feature was introduced. Annotations created on older videos will still function, but no new annotations are allowed. Mobile users will also be able to increase or decrease the pace of their videos. The developers are trying to find a way by which YouTube videos will seamlessly adapt to the size of the screen on any device. The ad content on the platform has also seen a major overhaul. If you want to monetize your channel, you need a minimum of 10,000 views on your video. Moderation tools have been added that allow channels to act on content that contains any specific words or phrases that they don't want on their videos.

Optimizing your Channel on YouTube

Before posting your first video, you have to optimize your channel. Your business may already have a YouTube channel, and you can still optimize it at any point. There are various steps involved in optimizing a YouTube channel.

Firstly, you have to understand the importance of SEO. The videos on your channel need to be optimized for SEO. This can be done by adding high-ranking keywords in the title of the video or using such keywords in the description of the video. You can also add relevant tags to the video so that it appears on the right searches. It is not necessary to choose between a keyword-y title and one that is catchy; you can integrate both. You can create a catchy title for your video and use a colon to add some keywords after it as well.

Ways to Grow your YouTube Channel

For successful content marketing, Videos are the key.

Most people are familiar with YouTube, which is a gallery of online videos, for regular users and even for professionals.

- Nearly 80% of online users watch YouTube video

- Google is the largest search engine in the world.

- One billion hours are being watched each day on YouTube.

Advertisements for businesses on YouTube are vital, particularly for marketing teams. Once you set up your YouTube channel, it is important for your business to seek more visibility for its YouTube videos.

In this section, you learn about strategies to adopt Google-friendly content and to multiply your YouTube channel.

Captivating Titles

Having a very good video is not the only requisite for making it a successful video. You need viewers who will watch the video. So, it becomes a strategy to elevate your video title with captivating titles to get more viewers.

Some tips for making a near-perfect YouTube title for more views are as follows:

- Finding the appropriate keywords: Keyword of the YouTube video title tells Google what the video is about. Meanwhile, it also tells the searching viewers the options it has in its server, so it's a double win situation.

- Keeping your video title as short as possible. Ideally, the length of video titles should be within 60 characters. It enables the viewers to see the whole title in a peep.

- Create descriptive titles that are clear: Do not make the viewers go through the hassle of figuring it out. Readers should know at a glance what the video is all about.

- Make the viewer realize why they even to watch the video. Everyone needs a reason to spend their time on the web and view any content. They will want to know how they will get benefited from it.

The plan to come up with a good title:

1. Define a gist of your video

2. Find short and descriptive keywords which tell the gist of your video

3. Finding an apt title which will be informative to viewers

Useful Resources

- SEO Ranking keyword suggestion tool for keyword research

- CoSchedule Headline Analyzer to analyze your titles

- Do not miss out on what's trending on YouTube to have an idea about the title

Create Perfect YouTube Thumbnails

Thumbnails will play a major role in attracting viewers to your content, so it should be related to your video content and title.

You can add a brief summary or image in your thumbnail to help viewers understand your content.

Make sure your thumbnail is customized in an attractive way, and it should interest your viewer enough to be curious about your content. Ideally, your thumbnail and title should complement each other.

Useful resources

- You can use Photoshop to customize your thumbnail

- Use AdWords to test your thumbnail

Limit Videos to Under 5 Minutes

Emphasize on the total watch time of your videos. The watch time of the majority of YouTube videos is not more than 5 minutes. This information is based on a ComScore survey. To make the best use of your videos, avoid repeating any topic. Making your video too long is not going to help either. Every viewer needs a good reason to spend time watching your video. You can decide the video content and duration to conclude what is better suited for your videos so that the viewers are engaged with it.

A few tips you should consider:

- Cut your video short; make it within 5 minutes

- High-quality content in each video sells better

- Make them short; meanwhile, keep it informative and interesting as well.

Useful Resources

Use YouTube Analytics to view what's best for your videos, and to get a closer look into the number of views, subscribers, watch time, and many more.

Branding Your Channel

Branding your channel is the next important thing you should consider. Make it look attractive and force your visitors to take you seriously. It increases brand awareness. Do put the Company logo for your channel.

41

For people to find you, add titles and descriptions to your videos. Near the banner photo, add the links to your website and social media. If you are mentioning some products in your video, you can also try to use self-branded overlays. Many people are unaware of this, but they will give you a chance to maintain your followers when they go through your videos.

It is also important to add an informative and relevant description of your company or your personality. Let people know what you are interested in and about the things that inspire you. Keep it short and engaging.

Useful Resources
Use Banner snacks to make online banner covers for your YouTube channel.

Include Call-to-Actions (CTAs)

By using calls to action in your videos, you get users to be more engaged on your YouTube channel. You have to know to use them wisely or else it can be quite irritating for people as well.

Know your goal, whether it is to acquire more likes or subscribers on your channel. You can always ask your viewers to subscribe to your channel at the end of the video or in between the video. You need to be smart and dedicated, and your efforts will be rewarded.

Useful Resources
The social blade helps you figure out channel size and also tells you who has the same audiences as you.

Share Videos via Social Media

Use the different social media platforms your business has profiles on for sharing your videos. It is essential if you want to grow your channel and reach many people. As a responsible marketer, it's important that you be active in social media, communities, and groups, not only to publish your latest videos.

Each platform for social media tends to have its own culture and methodology. You need to figure out the best culture to follow in the social media world and where your efforts will be noticed or appreciated.

Effective Tips to Promote Your Videos

- SlideShare presentations

- Pinterest and Twitter

- Make mini promo videos for your Facebook page and link back to your original YouTube video

- Integrate your videos in your blogs

- Use Scoop.it as a platform to publish your videos

- Promote and share the videos on relevant Facebook, LinkedIn communities and groups, and Google+

- Include your videos in some guest posts on related websites

- Insert your YouTube link on your Instagram bio

- Link your YouTube link to your Reddit for more views

Useful Resources

- Use the SE Ranking tool for social management to upload, schedule, and share your videos on social media platforms.

- To get more viewership, you can create YouTube badges for your site with YouTube API and link them back to your channel.

- Boosterberg allows you to promote your videos on Facebook, which can draw in more views.

Working with Other YouTubers

Collaborative, add-on videos are popular among the content creators. It's a better way to find new viewers and increase your subscriber base as well as views. It's also a double win strategy with the partner and viewers. Working with other familiar channels might make you look good by the association.

Ideas on How to Work with Others

1. Talk to your viewers: and ask what they want and what else they want to watch in the comments.

2. Find YouTube influencers and contact other brands in your field and try to make videos together.

3. Collaborate with popular YouTubers and brands.

4. It is not mandatory to work with a single brand or a person. You can be with few more at a time

5. Collaborate with other social network influencers.

It can help to grow your audience exponentially.

Useful Resources

To know the same audience as you, try Social Blade.

According to M.C Escher, "Only those who attempt the absurd will achieve the impossible."

To be a successful YouTuber, you need to experiment and understand what works for you and what does not and follow it throughout.

Your personality is reflected in how you stay true to your brand, video, or channel. Keep an eye on your channel/videos and see the effect it has on viewers.

Provide interesting, high-quality video content for your viewers. It will help grab their attention if you add captivating titles and thumbnails, stick to your word, and deliver what they want.

YouTube Ads for Beginners

Once you have created the perfect script with a storyboard and finished shooting and editing, you will get a brilliant video for your channel. Creating great videos takes a lot of time, effort, and resources. You cannot waste your efforts by merely uploading this video and hoping for views. YouTube is a great platform for great content to be discovered, but you cannot wait and depend on your luck. You need to be more proactive and do your best to increase the views and reach for your brand. YouTube ads can help you ensure that your content is viewed by your target audience.

Advertising is different on YouTube as compared to other platforms. It is not like a pay-per-click campaign or some paid social campaign.

There are creative constraints in place, and you have a lot of options to choose from as well. A basic understanding of YouTube advertising is required before you try creating ads for your business.

Certain changes have been made to AdWords in the last couple of years to ensure that advertisers are able to reach more viewers on YouTube. These changes are especially effective in reaching more viewers on mobile devices because this is where most of the user base lies. One of the changes was that you could use the Google search history of users to target viewers for your videos. You can target ads towards people according to certain products or services they may have searched for. When you open YouTube, you will probably be viewing ads similar to content that you have previously searched for. As you read on, you will understand a lot more about how YouTube ads work and how you can use them.

Types of Ads You Can Run on YouTube and the Various Formats Available

Like with other digital channels, you have to understand what counts as advertising on YouTube and what doesn't. The lines tend to blur between these two on YouTube, and it can be difficult for you to differentiate. Things like product placement tend to blur the lines here. However, there are certain methods that are considered advertising in a clear-cut way. The types of units that can be run on YouTube tend to change constantly. Keep checking for updates from YouTube's resources. Currently, the following are the types of ads that you can still run on YouTube:

- **Overlay ads**. These are semi-transparent ads that are shown at the bottom of videos.

- **Display ads.** These conventional ads are run on the right side of videos.

- **Skippable video ads**. These ads are run for 5 seconds, and then the viewer has the option of skipping the rest of the content or continuing to watch it before their video.

- **Non-skippable ads**. These ads cannot be skipped, and the viewer has to watch the whole ad before they can watch their chosen YouTube video.

- **Bumper ads**. These ads are also not skippable, but they only last for 6 seconds.

- **Sponsored cards**. These are ads that are displayed as text or display units while the chosen video is being played.

It might be a little confusing at first, but if you start using YouTube for a while, you will be able to differentiate between the types of ads. The difference between ads on YouTube and other platforms is that you can use skippable ads here. You may wonder why you would want viewers to skip your ads, but these are actually more cost-effective for marketing, and they also have better engagement rates.

Things to keep in mind while creating YouTube ads and figuring out what kind of ads work better on the platform.

You will find that many brands are uncomfortable with creating video ads for YouTube. However, this is not something you should shy away from. The main reason is; YouTube is a video platform, and this is the best place to share video content with people. Video ads will do better here than any other kind of ads like text units or display units.

So, what are the features you need to pay attention to in order to create a great YouTube ad? Well, there aren't any hard and fast rules for this. For higher engagement rates, you should just keep a few things in mind.

The first thing is that you should create an ad that has the viewer hooked as soon as they see it. You may create an ad in a skippable format, but if your content is good, they won't skip it. However, viewers can get distracted very easily, so you need to try and grab their attention as early as possible. Don't start the video with some lengthy introduction and sending across a brand message. The audio element of the video is just as important as the visual content. People often open separate tabs to keep YouTube videos playing in the background. This means that you can create a video that people might want to listen to while not watching as well. This is why you need to create a video that has visual and audio content that is engaging for viewers. Your ads need to be targeted at a specific audience too. If you don't have a target audience, your campaign won't make a lot of sense. Tailor the content according to the needs of your audience.

You may also have a question about how long your video should be. Well, there is no ideal length that we can suggest for your video. However, since it is an ad, it is better to keep it short and effective. A lengthy ad is more likely to make the user lose interest. A short ad will not be skipped as often as a lengthy ad is.

Targeting Options and Setting Targeting Parameters on a Campaign

An advantage of using YouTube advertising is that the platform seamlessly integrates data in detail on a massive scale. It gives brands the chance to use targeting. Demographics, behavior, interests, etc. are some of the aspects that you have to keep in mind while targeting an audience for your business. If you want to use all the targeting options, you need to utilize Google AdWords for your campaign. You may wonder why you should use AdWords for a YouTube campaign. However, it will be helpful because Google will help your business develop a campaign on a very wide outline range.

How to Check if the YouTube Ads are Working

Using Google AdWords allows you to use it to check the effectiveness of a campaign. The Video Campaigns tab in Google AdWords will help you check on how specific ad units are performing. Your dashboard will allow you to check many different metrics, and you can use the ones that are important for your ad. Some of the metrics include cookies, clicks, views, video viewership, etc.

Understanding the Different Types of YouTube Ads

Three types of video ads can be created for YouTube; Pre-roll, Bumpers, TrueView.

Pre-Roll Ads

Some in-stream ads on YouTube cannot be skipped. These either pay before the main video, after it or may even play during it. These Pre-roll ads are usually between 15-20 seconds long. When a video is longer than ten minutes, these ads can be played in between the video. You get as much freedom in these videos as you get on TrueView ads. Your content can include audio, dialogue, people, and other such elements that will help to represent your business to viewers. The pre-roll ads cannot be skipped, so you should optimize the attention of viewers using call-to-actions. Such ads will encourage viewers to click on the ad. Pre-roll ads are a good option if you want people to sign up for any events like a product launch. However, one thing to keep in mind while choosing this type of ad is that YouTube sells the space for these ads on a pay per click basis. Keeping this in mind, you need to make every click count for your ad.

TrueView Ads

TrueView ads are typical ads that are run on YouTube. As an advertiser, you will have to pay for your ad only when people watch it or interact with the ad. You can customize the ad for any type of content that you want. The advantage of this ad is that you will only have to pay for it if it is viewed for 30 seconds or more or if they take some specific action from that ad. A TrueView ad can be skippable or non-skippable. If you want the ad to be skippable, you need to make it at least 12 seconds long. The maximum length of such videos will be 6 minutes long. If you want a non-skippable ad, it should be at least 20 seconds long and not more. There are two types of TrueView ads that you can use:

Video Discovery Ads

Video Discovery Ads were earlier called in-display ads. These show up on the homepage of YouTube, on search results, and also in the section for related videos. If a user clicks on these ads, it will show the destination page with a companion banner display ad on the right side.

In-Stream Ads

This is the kind of ad that will play before the main video is run on YouTube. Viewers can skip these ads after it is run for five seconds. As an advertiser, you should make the first five seconds of these videos count so that viewers want to watch the rest of it. These ads can also be played on the Google Display Network and other sites that will have Google video ad space. The marketer will be able to customize this kind of ad using overlay texts and call-to-actions.

TrueView campaigns may include music, dialogues, or people. Such campaigns should not be used for making regular promotions. You can work on creating ads that will appeal to the users such that they don't want to skip it. Testimonials and case studies that invoke empathy among viewers can be used for such ads. If your ad is memorable, people will not want to skip the ad. Such ads can go viral quite quickly as well. TrueView ads also provide marketers with a lot of information about the ads they run. This kind of information will help optimize ads that you run in the future.

Bumpers

The shortest kind of YouTube ad is a Bumper. Such ads are run for six seconds only and are played before the main video is run. It can be challenging for marketers to use six seconds to tell a complete story. However, these are a good element to add to larger campaigns. If you can create content while making every second count, these ads will be effective for your brand. Another advantage is that viewers don't usually skip these ads since they are so short.

Setting Up and Launching a Video Advertising Campaign

After creating a video ad, you have to devise a campaign for it. Firstly, you need to use Google AdWords to set the campaign up. Select the type of campaign you want from the drop-down menu in the +Campaign option. Then enter a name for your campaign and select video as the option from type. You can then select from In-Stream ads and Video discovery ads. You also have to set up a daily budget for your ad. You can choose from standard or accelerated delivery for the ad. Standard delivery ads will be displayed in an even manner throughout the day. Accelerated delivery ads will provide you with views as quickly as possible. To capitalize on any current trend, you should use the help of accelerated delivery ads.

You also have to decide what networks to display your ads on. YouTube search and YouTube videos are the two options you can choose from. On the YouTube search, the ad will appear on the homepage as well as on search results. In the case of YouTube videos, the ads will show before or around videos shown on GDN. Your campaigns for YouTube videos and Search have to be created differently. This will help you track performance more efficiently. You also need to specify the location of your target audience to display the ads. You can also use AdWords to specify language, operating system, carrier, and device. The bid can be increased or decreased depending on if the ad is shown on mobile devices or others. There are many other parameters in the advanced settings that can be manipulated for increasing ROI for your ad. For example, you can customize a schedule for showing the ads and decide start or end dates for running it. You also have to select the maximum amount you want to pay for views, and this can be adjusted. Your ads will be suitable for certain audiences only, so you need to define the target audience. Be careful while doing this because your ads will be of no use when shown to the wrong audience. Combining keyword targeting and in-display ads will be a powerful tool. You should do sufficient research and test out keywords so that it helps gain more views, clicks, and conversions. The ad can be re-marketed to people who may already be in contact with your business. It will make re-engagement more likely when it comes to people who are already familiar with your business. Link your YouTube channel where the video is hosted with your account on AdWords. Once you click on "Finish," you can run the ad campaign.

Chapter Six

Facebook Marketing 101

If you're getting started with social media marketing, it is imperative to be on Facebook. Facebook has more than 2 billion users active from around the world. It began as a photo-sharing website for some college kids but has now grown into a significant player in the business world. What you need to be concerned with is the fact that there are great marketing opportunities on this social network, and it is worth your time and effort.

Before you start marketing on Facebook, you might stop to wonder if your customers are even on Facebook. The answer to this is probably yes because users of all ages and from most places around the world tend to use social media these days, and Facebook is at the top of the list. So, no matter what age group your business might be targeting, they are probably on Facebook. This is why your business needs to have an active profile on Facebook as soon as possible.

Let's look at how you can get set up and running on Facebook to carry out a successful social media marketing campaign.

Tools on Facebook That are Useful for Marketing

Facebook Pages
The most obvious marketing tool to use on Facebook is Facebook Pages. It is like a personal profile but for your business and will have

all the information that users might want to know. A Facebook Page can be created for anything from a brand, company, and service to a celebrity. When users "Like" or "Follow" the Facebook page, they automatically start getting updates on it on their news feed. However, users will probably have to click on the option for viewing posts first if they want to see instant updates. This is a tactic by Facebook to encourage the page owner to pay for higher visibility. If you don't want to pay for it, encourage users to follow your page so that they see the posts. It saves you a lot of money this way. However, the charges for boosting a post are also not very high, so that most businesses can afford it.

You may wonder what the difference between a Facebook Page and profile is. One key difference is that if you want to connect with someone through their personal profile, you have to send a friend request, and they would have to accept it. A Facebook page just has to be liked and followed without requiring any approval from the owner of the page. Another difference is that there is a limit on the number of friends someone can have on their personal profile. A Facebook page can have endless likes and followers. The latter is a better option for a business.

Facebook pages are free and also quite easy to create. Anyone can create a decent Facebook page in 10 minutes. Getting the likes and follows is what will require more time.

Tips for a Good Facebook Page
- Set up your brand logo as the profile photo and make sure it is a high-quality image. Your cover photo can act as a backstory for your brand, so use pictures of your employees or products and services.

- The About section should tell every visitor what your business is about in a short but precise way. Include information like what your business does, where it is set up, and how people can contact you.

- Post content that your followers will actually want to see on their news feed. Don't keep promoting a product endlessly and don't post too often. Instead, post helpful content that will make your audience look forward to more posts. Post about new product announcements, coupon codes, blog posts, or videos that your audience will enjoy. If you spam their feed, then you will lose followers quicker than you got them.

- Use Facebook Insights to study your page statistics. It will help you understand what kind of posts people like more and what kind of content you need to avoid.

Facebook Groups

Facebook groups have been around for quite a while. However, they now let you create groups based on brands. If you create a Facebook page for your brand, you can create a group associated with it. You have more control over the group once you attach the brand to it. These groups are similar to forums for discussions, but they have features like personal profiles or pages. The group can help you reach out to any potential customers related to your industry. Facebook groups are also free, and these tend to have a high amount of engagement. However, the only downside is the amount of time it consumes. Running a Facebook page is fairly simple and only requires you to check in a time or two in the day. However, groups require constant monitoring and activity.

Facebook Marketplace

Facebook marketplace is a game-changer for any business looking to sell products via Facebook. This marketplace is a little similar to Craigslist but is a part of Facebook. Since this feature is relatively new, it is constantly being revised. However, it has a lot of potential for any product-based business. Set up a shop if you want to sell products. Your Facebook Page will have a separate tab called "Shop" where you can list the products that you want to sell. Once your products are listed, anyone on Facebook can search for them. Using the Facebook Marketplace is a must for anyone in eCommerce.

Facebook Jobs

Facebook also has the option of posting jobs. Facebook jobs also feature relatively new, among others. It is not necessarily about marketing but is worth mentioning because it can help you reach out to potential employees when there is an opening. This is a feature that you can utilize while growing your company and enlisting more employees.

Targeted Advertising

The advertising platform on Facebook is one of the prime advantages of Facebook marketing. It allows you to create ads that are target based. You can target people from a specific geographical location, of any age group, any level of education, and even those who use specific devices. Users have the option of hiding any ads they don't like, or else they may choose to "Like" the page beneath an ad they like. Since Facebook gathers a lot of demographic information from its users, it tends to have a better target-based advertising program compared to others. Users can be targeted based on most things that you might find on their profiles. It also allows you to track the success of your ads with any segment. Facebook ads can run on the basis of impressions or clicks. Facebook will also show you bids for ads that are similar to the ones you post. This will show you if your ad bid is similar to those in the same industry. Another helpful feature is that you can stay within your budget by setting a daily limit. Compared to Facebook Pages or Groups, you will get more success with Facebook ads. Facebook advertising is a very powerful tool that can help your business reach more consumers and grow in size. The only advantage the groups and pages have over ads is that they are free while ads will cost you money.

Facebook Ads have different subtypes to choose from. You can choose from leads, canvas, offers, video, and many others. Every type of ad has its own advantage, and you can choose the subtype depending on the type of marketing campaign you are running. Studying the ads run by your competitors will help you decide on the type of ad you should run. You can do this by going to the Facebook Page of any competing company and clicking on the "Info and Ads" tab there. It will display all their active ads under that tab. If you are the administrator of a page, you can create ad campaigns for it. You can also access the Ad Manager, but this tool is a little complicated for beginners to use. Starting out with the basic features will let you understand how to use the Ad Manager soon as well.

The targeting tools on Facebook are very useful for a marketing campaign. Users can be targeted using virtually any information they might have added on their profile. If you want to target on the basis of location, you can specify everything from the city, zip code, and state to country. Local businesses will find this feature particularly useful as they can target their ads to people in their vicinity. You can also choose any basic demographics like age, relationship status, etc. Ads can also be targeted towards people who may have just moved from one place to another. This means you can target potential new customers in your area. People can also be targeted on the basis of their interests. So, if you have a gym and hold martial arts classes, you can target people with this interest to join your gym. If you sell products related to a particular sport, you can target people who like that sport. The Ad Manager will also allow you to target people whose email addresses you may have. You can create a private list with these emails and target your ads towards them.

For anyone looking to create a tightly targeted ad, you have the option to create ads differently for any different demographics. A tightly targeted ad will give you better results. If you want to target people based on their interests, Facebook provides you with the information required to help you do so. If you have a bookshop, you can target ads towards people based on the books they like. Create an ad with a particular book and target it towards people who have mentioned that book in their interests. Similarly, you can have different ads with different books for different groups of people.

Facebook Exchange allows any business to take advantage of the retargeting feature with real-time bidding. Targeting can be done on the basis of the user's web history. If a user has visited a particular product page on the website but does not make a purchase, that retailer can use that product in an advertisement targeting that customer. Previously, the retargeting ads were confined to the side column on the Facebook page. However, they are not appearing in the user's news feed itself and is thus a valuable asset for businesses. Ad placements on the side column do not see as much response as the ads that appear on the news feed.

Sponsored Stories

Sponsored stories are ads that show users interactions. It is based on the marketing concept of "Word of mouth." When users see that a page has been liked by some of their friends, they are more inclined to like that page as well. The goal of the Sponsored Stories feature is to have users take actions similar to their friends. You can place an ad and show the user, which of their friends have liked your page, or how many of them have claimed an offer you posted. This action taken by their friends prompts them to act similarly as well. Sponsored Stories are given preferred positioning and are the only ad format that is available on any mobile device. The Facebook ad create flow allows you to create Facebook Sponsored Stories.

It is evident that Facebook is a powerful marketing tool that is flexible for its users. Regardless of what kind of business you have, Facebook has many different marketing options that you can tailor towards your needs. It can be customized according to any type of business, budget, or time factor. It will take a little time to get familiar with all the different features that Facebook offers for marketing, but the effort will be worth it. Facebook has grown rapidly since its beginning and is still growing further. This provides a lot of opportunities for businesses on Facebook. Facebook marketing is an indispensable part of any social media marketing campaign. Take out time to try and test a few different campaigns on Facebook to find what works best for your company.

How to Get Likes and Fans on Facebook

Once you have created your Facebook business page, you need it to become successful. Success will be measured differently for different people based on their goals. However, the basic focus should be on building brand awareness, driving more sales, launching products, and collecting leads. One of the first things to focus on is to get more "Likes" for your Page. When a user likes your Page, they choose to see updates from your Page on their news feed. It is important to figure out a way to get more likes on your Facebook page to help your campaigns be successful.

Avoid Buying Likes

A lot of people choose the easy way to put into getting more likes and just paying for it. You can easily Google search and find services that provide you with instant likes for a certain fee. You can even customize the number of likes you want according to how much you are willing to pay. This may make your Page look instantly successful, but it won't necessarily be successful at all despite all those paid-for likes. This is not the right way to master Facebook marketing. The likes that you can get via these services tend to come from fake accounts, click farms, or even hacked accounts. This means that despite these user accounts liking your Page, it will not lead to any engagement or conversions for your business. This means that you would just have wasted your money on those likes. You also have to remember that all Facebook posts don't necessarily show up on the News Feed. A particular algorithm is used to look at engagement rates, and this determines what is included on the News Feed. When the number of likes and comments lack on your posts, your content is not likely to be visible because your Page may have a lot of likes, but the fake accounts are not going to engage in any of your content posts.

Any real users who come across your Page will also question the discrepancy that is visible. You should also be aware that Facebook has a team that checks for any such suspicious behavior on their user accounts. They have the right to shut down any account that displays such behavior. This should be enough to scare you away from any such tactic to buy likes.

Understand How to Get Likes

Focus on how to get likes in the right way for your Page. This can be done by promoting your page on Facebook and getting more visibility. As we have mentioned before, the "About" section in your business' Facebook Page should be filled out carefully. The description should include searchable information in an organic way. Let people know what your business is about and what it offers to people. When you are building a new page, share it with all your existing friends on Facebook. People who know you are more likely to support your business at first. Don't over-promote it to people who might not have any interest in it at all. Encourage your friends and colleagues to share the Page with their circle as well. You can tell any employees who deal with a lot of people to share the Page with them. Nonetheless, the best way to gain more likes is to be active and build an engaging community. Posting helpful and interesting content will make new users want to like or share your content or Page with others. It is also important to be responsive to people, so reply to any messages or comments as often and quickly as possible. Facebook provides a green badge saying "Very responsive" to any page that is interactive and responsive to users.

Promote Your Page

Use your website to promote your Facebook Page. Don't focus solely on promoting your Page on Facebook. You can use other social media and your own website to promote your Page as well. Add follow buttons linking to your Page on your website as well as your blog. This will allow visitors to follow your Facebook Page even when they visit your website or blog. Page plugins can be used easily to do this.

Use email contacts and promote your Page to existing customers as well. If you have a local setup, use creative ways to promote your Facebook page to customers. You can place a poster or placard with a Facebook sticker and the name of your Page on it. Ask people to like and share. You can also add a custom URL to any receipts you hand out. At the checkout counter, you can let customers know about your Facebook presence and offer a discount for liking or sharing the Page. Everyone loves a good incentive. Even if you don't have a brick and mortar setup, you can add links to your Facebook page on any receipts, updates, or emails.

You can also use your other social media accounts to promote your Facebook page. However, you should do this sparingly and discreetly. Don't annoy your audience by pushing them to do this. Just add a button linking to your Facebook page or add links to your Page in some of your content or in your "About" info.

How to Create an Effective Facebook Marketing Strategy

Facebook allows you to post many different kinds of content. Posting content is fairly simple, but what is more important is when and what you post. This is the main challenge you will face while marketing on Facebook. For a successful marketing strategy on Facebook, you need first to understand your audience better. Then you have to develop the right kind of content to drive real results. The next step would be to schedule posts into your calendar. You will also have to keep checking for any new offerings from Facebook to connect with prospects.

Identify your Facebook Audience

Take some time to evaluate the buyer personas at large. By buyer persona, we mean a generalized representation of the ideal customers for your business. This will allow you to determine the Facebook audience you want to target. It is useful to determine buyer personas regardless of which department you work in - sales, marketing, services, or product development. This is because it helps to relate better to any target customers. Similarly, when you understand the challenges or goals of your buyer personas on Facebook, it will allow you to determine the kind of content you should post. You will be able to tweak the positioning accordingly as well. Interview a mix of customers, referrals, and prospects to build the buyer persona. Gauge the knowledge they have of your industry and what are the biggest challenges they face. Also, find out their goals and what they use to learn or develop their skills. Check the Facebook pages of your competitors to evaluate their post frequency, content mix, visual quality, engagement, and response time. The ads platform on Facebook has a free tool called Audience Insights. You can use this to get a better understanding of your audience. This tool can be used even without deploying an ad. It will allow you to obtain data about your audience and also your competitors' audience. Once you dig into this tool, you will see a lot of information from location to engagement frequency. It will be valuable in determining your target audience on Facebook.

Schedule Posts for Your Social Media Calendar

If you use social media for marketing, you will have to juggle many tasks on a daily basis. This will include posting content across the various social media channels you use, responding to any messages or comments from customers, monitoring activity, etc. This means you will have quite a lot of tasks to be accomplished on a daily basis. This is why you need to prepare content from before and have it ready to be posted. You cannot scramble to create some new posts at the end moment. Using a calendar for social media content is the best way to keep up. You can use a spreadsheet to write out any posts in advance and create slots to post them on specific days and timings. This will prevent any last moment of stress and improve efficiency in managing your social media marketing campaign. It will also help you organize tracking links and make it easy for you to evaluate any mix of formats or topics. Create tabs on the spreadsheet for all the social media platforms you use. Break the schedule down on a daily basis with time slots. You should also have a monthly view of plotting out large campaigns. Scheduling posts makes your work much easier in the long run. Multiple resources are available to help you schedule posts and automate posting. Facebook itself has the option of scheduling a post. When you create a post on Facebook, instead of clicking on "Share Now" click on the small arrow near it and choose "Schedule." You can then select the time and date for when you want the content to be posted. The "Publishing Tools" tab in the menu of your Facebook Page will allow you to manage all scheduled posts.

You also have to find the best times that you should be posting on Facebook. You have to decide on how often you should post and also at what time. There is no fixed answer to this that will apply to everyone in general. It depends on your industry, region, target audience, goals, etc. All of this has to be factored into determining when you post so that more people view the post. However, in general, you can post between 1–4 p.m. on weekdays and 12–1 p.m. on weekends. These timings generally work for most Facebook pages. If you consider how often you should post, the rule of thumb is to focus on quality and not quantity. Don't post too often and spam the news feed of your followers. Be selective about the kind of content you post so that you don't overwhelm your followers. Instead of wasting time on creating many posts, spend time on creating something that would be highly engaging.

Generate Leads on Facebook

Facebook marketing goals vary according to the type of business and the kind of content published. Most of the content posted on your Page will gain more views or create awareness. But you can also use Facebook to get actual leads for your business. A lead is a person interested in the product or service your company offers. They show interest by giving you some of their information by filling out a form or requesting a sample or demo. To convert viewers from your Page to paying customers, you have to post content that will direct to forms strategically. For example, you can set up an offer on your landing page that can only be claimed if they sign up or fill some form. You can also create videos that will promote any lead generation offers. Facebook events can be used for upcoming webinars. However, all your content should not be about lead generation. Just mix the content together to get the best results. Facebook Lead Ads can also be used for capturing lead information. This way, you can avoid any landing page friction or any click-through path that is longer. Customers can use this feature to access offers from your Page without having to exit the Facebook app.

Facebook Analytics for Tracking and Measuring Results

By now, you have launched a great Facebook Page for your business and given its personality with good content. You know how to gain more likes on your Page and content and also might have created a strategy to appeal to a wider audience. But how do you find out how you are really doing? You cannot carry out marketing successfully without tracking and measuring the results of your campaign. Guesswork will only lead to underperformance. Instead, you can use the analytical tools that Facebook offers.

Page Insights

At the top of your Facebook Page, you will see a menu with "Insights." Clicking on this will show you an "Overview" of the important activity that took place in your Page in the last seven days.

Likes

The "Likes" tab in the left vertical navigation bar will show you the number of likes you gain or lose in a day. A graph with "Net Likes" will show you how many likes you have when you deduct the number of unlikes from the number of likes on that day. The "Benchmark" section will help you compare the average performance on your Page over time.

Reach

The "Reach" tab will show you how many people your post reached. This will be broken down into organic reach and traffic generated from pay. When a post gets more likes, shares, or comments, it is more likely to show up on people's feed. It will show up less if more people mark it as spam or hide the post. When there is a spike in the Reach graph, click on it to see what content caused the surge in engagement.

Page Views

This helps you see how people reached your Page and also where they go from your Page. The "Top Sources" graph will show you the external referrers that bring your Page a lot of traffic. It could be a search engine, blog, or website.

Posts

The "Posts" tab under Page Insights is the most useful one for marketers. The top will have a graph that shows when your users are online. This information will help you determine when you should post your content so you can use it for scheduling your social media posts. There will also be a record of all the posts you published on your Page. This will be arranged in reverse chronological order and will include core metrics. You will be able to understand the kind of content that engages your audience more and what doesn't.

Post Details

Page Insights will be useful for monthly reporting. However, you also need to check on a single post at times to see its performance. Above the "Like" button, click on the "people reached" number to see post details. You won't have to go to Page Insights just to check the performance of a single post. There are in-depth metrics available here for video content as well. You can view the average watch time here too.

Facebook Reactions

"Reactions" is a relatively new feature that was introduced in 2016. It allows users to react to a post using the emojis available. It's not just about getting likes anymore. However, when a person reacts to your post, it still counts as alike. In Post Details, you will be able to see a breakdown of all reactions. This will allow you to get an insight into what your audience thinks of your content. The customers who leave a "Love" on your post are usually fans of your business.

Social ROI

When you spend time and effort on your campaign, you will want to check if it is paying off. It is like checking your return on investment for your social media campaign. Before tracking social ROI, you have to set some goals. Some of the key performance indicators are views, lead generation, or engagement. You should also use tracking links that have UTM parameters when you post any links on Facebook. Certain marketing automation platforms will help you create such links directly, assign them to campaigns, and track how many clicks you get. Closed-loop reporting from a marketing automation software allows you to see which of your posts are creating real impact in terms of customers and leads. You can then be more confident in decision making for your social media campaign.

How to Start Advertising on Facebook

To start advertising on Facebook, you will have to check off many boxes. For instance, is the copy engaging, or are you targeting the right audience? You also have to think about how much you should be spending. Facebook advertising can often be too overwhelming for beginners, and this prevents many from even trying it. However, the platform has so many users that it offers a real opportunity for anyone looking to drive brand awareness. It also gives you the chance to get a lot more leads than you could from other channels. This is why you should try and use Facebook advertising for your business.

Creating a Facebook Ad Campaign

Before you start advertising, you have to understand the terms related to it. There are three main elements involved in Facebook advertising:

- **Campaigns.** These include all assets.

- **Ad sets**. These are groups of ads that you will be targeted at specific audiences. For separate audience groups, you need separate ad sets.

- **Ads.** These are the individual ads that you will be posting on Facebook.

Facebook has two editing choices available for use while creating an advertisement - Ad Manager and Power Editor. Most companies find the Ad Manager useful while large advertisers prefer using Power Editor because it helps control many campaigns.

You can start with Facebook advertising using the Ads Manager.

- First, choose an objective for your ad. These will fall under three categories - consideration, conversion, or awareness. Then define the audience that you want to target your ad towards. You can specify any demographics while targeting an audience. You can also choose an audience that might have liked a similar page or business.

- The next step is to determine the budget for running this ad. You can select a daily budget and also a lifetime budget. The daily budget is how much you are willing to spend on a single day. The lifetime budget is how much you are willing to spend in total over a period of time, and Facebook will then divide this equally on a daily basis.

- Then set a schedule for the ad set. You can choose to start running your ad immediately or during a specific time and period in the future.

After you designate the campaign, you can create an ad.

- Choose from the two ad formats that Facebook gives you options for.

- Then upload any creative assets and add a clickable headline for the ad. You have to decide how you want the ad to look. You will be given certain recommendations for designs, image size, etc. Remember that Facebook prefers images that have minimal text. When your image has too much text, it will receive very little delivery.

- Tweak the text on your ad and then preview the whole ad for viewers on desktops or mobile devices. If you are satisfied with it, you can place the order.

Use the Facebook Ad Manager to check how your ad is performing from time to time. You need to pay attention to a few metrics while your ad is running:

- Actions.

- Cost per action.

- Frequency.

You can even export this data for future use.

Once you create a good marketing campaign for your business on Facebook, you have to put it to work. Remember that there is a lot of competition so your business must stand out in order to be noticed. Be deliberate and be helpful to your audience. The tools available on Facebook make it easy for your business to develop a real relationship with its customers. Utilize it well and watch your business grow on Facebook.

Chapter Seven

Twitter Marketing 101

Twitter is an amazing platform that allows anyone interested in expanding their business in giving it recognition in all parts of the world. However, Twitter is extremely fast-paced and provides very limited space and time for promotion, unlike Facebook and Instagram, where a post has a shelf life that is five times longer than that of Tweets. More than 7000 tweets are updated every second, and so the average lifecycle of one tweet is approximately 19 minutes.

This is a disadvantage a tweet may have from having a recognizable or desired impact as it is very likely that the tweet may get lost among the thousands of other tweets that are updated every second. Your technique for marketing should be relevant enough to catch anyone's attention and pique their interest. It may be slightly difficult to find what works and what doesn't, but keeping an organized, calm, and concentrated mind is the first step to creating a Twitter marketing strategy. This strategy must be firm and crafted in such a way so that it can act as the foundation for your success. You must be sure of your definition of success and set their goals accordingly, all the while benchmarking the current status of the brand's performance, including that of their teams. This will act as a measurement of progress so one may keep track of how well the strategy is working and if it is producing desirable results for the business. When one has identified the target audience, the focus should be on bringing values that may really help them out and encourage them to keep associating with the business and become faithful customers or consumers of one's products or services.

Using Twitter for Business

Create the Right Handle

The right Twitter handle, display picture, and header image play a vital role. It should be simple and easy to keep in mind because it will act as a guide for people to remember the business. The name of the business should remain consistent on all social media platforms and must contain simple characters, especially the Twitter handle because that is how people will be searching up your brand name. Numbers and punctuation marks will only cause inconvenience and should be avoided at all costs. You want to keep short and memorable. Because of how popular shopping online and browsing is, consumers will prefer to interact with the brand's Twitter account instead of physically visiting the store or location.

Logos are a must because that is how people can recognize your brand even if they do not remember the name. It will also build awareness for your brand, and every time a customer goes to your Twitter page, they will eventually become familiar with it and recognize it anywhere they go if they see it. Sticking to clear logos is better so that it may be recognizable even when it is compressed (as people may go online on different sized electronic devices) and use it as the display photo. Headshots as display pictures are an option for personal businesses or brands.

The header space is most likely the first thing a person sees when they go to your profile and so it can also be used for promoting your brand and showing off what it has to offer to consumers from all over the world. Your bio must also blend in with all the other features of your Twitter account. It must be optimized to showcase the personality of your business or brand. It doesn't have to be complicated, but it has to be done in the best type of way. All one needs to do is to explain who they are and what they stand for. The bio must be accurate, must have personality, and be original. Showcasing what the brand has achieved throughout its lifetime is also a neat way to pull in interests from consumers as everybody likes to see and interact with brands that have accomplishments under their belt. And most importantly, it must be most relevant to the target audience. Any other brands or businesses that have worked with your own must be tagged in this given space.

Determine the Right Time to Tweet

There are particular times during the day and days of the week when the number of users' peaks into activity. These particular times must be kept in mind, as people are most likely to interact with one's brand. It will help to advance your impressions, gaining tons, and tons of click and boost engagements. The weekend, including Friday, have higher CTRs than anything that is posted during the weekdays. As for the time of day when people are most active on Twitter, it is advisable to tweet during the hours between 12 P.M.-8 P.M. But even better to test out what time of the day works best to attract your target audience. Once that is settled, you can set posts to go live during peak hours.

Use Hashtags

Hashtags are one of the more useful tools when it comes to Twitter, and you must be careful not to overwhelm one's audience with one too many hashtags. They should be kept simple, clear, and its uses must be kept minimal. Any tweet that contains hashtags get double the amount of engagement and recognition, but too many hashtags may result in the opposite. Overuse must be avoided, and context must be provided to your posts through them. Twitter's advanced search option helps one get feedback and find potential customers to add to the already existing numbers of clients and finding out new leads for your business.

Pay Attention to Visuals

Because sight is the best-selling sense, visual representation of your brand must be appealing and so adding images to your tweet, you may bring in more clicks and subscriptions. These images have to be on-brand, keep up with the trends, be relevant, and of fairly high quality. Selling products this way is highly efficient and very popular these days. Videos are also considered to be even more pleasing to watch, and Twitter allows for this option as well. The Live video option is also available and is uploaded as tweets for a longer lifespan for your followers to enjoy whenever they want to.

Interact More

Interaction with your followers is one of the key components for gaining a faithful audience. Make sure to do things that allows for more interacting between them, find out what piques their interest like making polls and doing Q&As, making sure to have a forum where visitors and potential customers can leave any and all types of comments, follow and network, retweet, use @mentions and tag them and never be afraid to ask for help. Any feedback is good for growth within the brand. Reaching out to influencers with large followings is also another way of good promotion. These influencers can then promote your brand as long as their posts align with the message that your brand wants to convey. This will drive traffic to your website. Twitter ads, albeit expensive, is the fastest way to boost your brand's engagements and increase influence. Hosting chats on Twitter is a great way to build community and loyalty. Using hashtags, people can meet online to discuss different topics, share their thoughts and ideas, and keep up with the news. Twitter also has the option "Moments," where the day's biggest tweet where interaction peaked can be shared like collaborations with major influencers.

Keep an Eye on Competitors

When you have a business to run, it is always best to keep your eyes on your competitors. The world is a big place filled with big brands in countless numbers that are doing similar things like you are, fairly well, in fact. So, follow them and check up on what they are sharing with their Twitter audience. Use your Twitter analytics to keep up with your performance on the platform, track your followers' activity demographics, and see how your ads are performing.

Create a Twitter List

Twitter Lists are organized groups of Twitter accounts that you select and then put together under specific categories. Any user can create or view a Twitter List. You can make a list called Marketing Experts for popular marketing leaders that you follow. Similarly, you can create many such lists for all the accounts that you follow to help identify their category. On opening any of these Twitter Lists, you will only be viewing tweets from the accounts that are under those lists. For someone who wants to follow only a few specific accounts, Twitter Lists are a great option. These lists will help you to review posts, content, and interactions more easily.

Host a Twitter Chat

Another great way to engage followers is hosting a Twitter chat. Schedule a Twitter chat to discuss a topic and ask your audience if they have any questions or opinions to share. This will help to create a sense of community among your audience. You have to choose a topic and then set a date and time for hosting the Twitter Chat. You should also create a specific hashtag for that chat. Share all of this information with the followers you have on Twitter and also on other social media. Everyone who wants to view your chat or participate in it will have to use the unique hashtag that you shared. By searching for the hashtag, they will be able to see all the responses, comments, or questions related to the topic on your Twitter chat. They can also share their own thoughts or comments by using the hashtag. A Twitter Chat will encourage interaction on your profile and make more people talk about your business. The chat acts as a more personal experience between the business and its audience.

Advertise on Twitter

Using Twitter for advertising is another great way to reach a bigger audience. Advertising on Twitter will make your content easily discoverable by people and thus help you to increase your following and influence a lot more. Twitter Ads or promoted tweets can be used for this purpose.

Promoted Tweets

This means your tweet will appear on Twitter streams or in the search results for specific Twitter users. It helps you to get a lot of people on specific webpages. To promote a tweet, you have to pay a monthly fee for the duration of its run. Promoted tweets will be put in daily campaigns by Twitter, and they will target the audience that you want for your business. This target audience can be specified in your settings when you set it up. Twitter users can engage or interact on Twitter ads the same way that they do in a normal tweet.

Twitter Ads

If you have a specific goal for your business and want to use different kinds of tweets, Twitter Ads are a great option. It is ideal for those who want to grow their follower base and want to see a significant increase in brand awareness. You can choose from different objectives like video views, app installs, or website conversions when you are using Twitter Ads. Your decisions regarding the objectives of the ads will determine the price you will have to pay for running the ad.

Drive Website Traffic

You can use Twitter to direct traffic to your business website in a number of ways. You can add the URL of the website to your Twitter profile. You can also add links to any blogs or web pages in your tweets. To drive traffic to your website, add the URL of the website on the bio section in your profile. You should also retweet any content that has direct links to your website. Use a Twitter Timeline to embed a tweet on your website. You can use Twitter Ads to drive traffic to specific landing pages as well.

Twitter Moments

Twitter Moments include tweets on a specific event or topic. It is similar to a "best of" collection on any topic. You can create a section of Twitter Moments for your followers or use the ones that are already there, such as News, Fun, and Entertainment. Twitter Moments can be organized into a collection of tweets to help market events or campaigns you are running. They are helpful in social media marketing because they provide a way to promote any event or topic related to your business in an engaging way. It helps you to show a specific brand image to the audience on Twitter.

Get Verified

Depending on the size of your business, you may choose to try and get your profile verified on Twitter. According to Twitter, you will only get a verified account if your business falls under music, fashion, acting, government, religion, politics, media, journalism, business, sports, and such key interest areas. You can apply for the verification badge, and Twitter will decide if your profile gets verified. If they accept the application, a blue check badge will be added to your Twitter handle. This is how Twitter shows people that your account is authentic. A verified account helps other users to be sure of who they are following, and it helps to differentiate the account from that of an impersonator. There are many accounts that have similar handles, usernames, or content. It can be difficult for the layman to differentiate and identify which account really belongs to your business. Since Twitter does the authentication process, the blue tick establishes your business as one that is trustworthy and legitimate.

Increase Follower Count

You have to focus on increasing your follower count as much as possible. The more followers your business has, the more attention it will get from people. It will allow an increase in views and more interaction surrounding your brand. You will also be able to direct more traffic to your website through Twitter.

The following tips will help you get more followers on Twitter fast:

- Make your content shareable

- Create content that is engaging like a contest, survey or giveaway

- Enlist the help of influencers on Twitter

- Add links on your website to connect people to your Twitter profile

- Interact often with the followers you have and try to encourage loyalty

All of the above points are ways to use Twitter for business.

Marketing tips for Twitter

How to Improve your Twitter Marketing Strategy

Use Keyword Targeting in Twitter Ads

Keyword targeting is an important component of Twitter ads. It helps to engage users on Twitter by using certain words or phrases that you use in your content or that they search for on Twitter. It will help you to reach your target audience exactly when your business or content is relevant to them. Twitter keyword targeting is of two types.

Search Keyword Targeting

This will help your tweets show up when a user searches for the topics that you associate with your business. For instance, if you sell sports equipment, you can target users who search for tweets about sports, fitness, equipment, gear, or health.

Timeline Keyword Targeting

This will help you to act on specific actions, feelings, thoughts, or emotions of your users once they have tweeted about it. For instance, as a sports equipment company, you can target phrases or keywords on tweets with "weight loss tips" or "home gym."

Implement Hashtags

Tweets without hashtags actually get only half the engagement that tweets with hashtags get. This gives you a clear idea about the importance of using hashtags. When you use hashtags in your tweets, it helps increase your Twitter influence. While we encourage the use of hashtags, you also have to keep a few things in mind while doing so. Your hashtags have to be such that they help you reach the target audience that will benefit your business.

- Create a unique hashtag for your business. This will help any followers or target audience to find your Twitter account or tweets easily.

- Create unique hashtags for any other group of tweets so that they are memorable and relevant. Such hashtags will help carry out any campaign you are running.

- Utilize Twitter analytics to identify the most successful hashtags you have used. You can then use these hashtags more often in your future tweets.

- Avoid using too many hashtags. While hashtags are effective, overusing them will work the opposite way. If users see your tweets with more than two or three relevant hashtags, they will be unlikely to engage with you. Tweets with one or two great hashtags see a lot more engagement in general.

Establish a Schedule for Sharing Content

It is important to post on a regular basis while you establish a following for your Twitter account. It will help to maintain engagement on your account and thus attract more followers. You have to tweet on a regular basis and also figure out the right times of the day to tweet at. If you are a B2C company, it is better to tweet on the weekends. If you are a B2B company, it is better for you to tweet on weekdays.

When it comes to the frequency of posting, there isn't any specific rule to follow on Twitter. You can tweet quite often, but you should only post content that is meaningful and has a purpose. Don't post random tweets just for the sake of tweeting. If you spam user's feed with meaningless tweets, they will unfollow your account. Twitter analytics will help you determine the times when you should post as well. You will be able to check how your users respond to frequent tweets or when you tweet only a couple of times. If they engage more when you tweet less, you should follow that pattern in the future. Similarly, if your audience likes it when you tweet frequently, share some good tweets more often. Social media management tools will help you create a schedule for tweeting once you have determined when you want to post. Such tools will help you create your tweets in advance and schedule them for posting at specific times.

Create a Twitter Campaign

Marketing campaigns are a great way for you to reach your target audience and drive more sales. If you create a profile on Twitter, you should also create a specific campaign for it. It will help you target users and increase your following while increasing brand awareness.

Use the following tips for creating a Twitter marketing campaign:

- Do research on your competition

- Figure out a way to appeal to the target audience for your business

- Decide on the kind of content you want to create

- Share and promote the content you create

- Analyze performance

Create a Strong Bio

It is crucial to create a bio that is strong and memorable for your Twitter profile. Any visitor on your profile will first view the bio you set up. This will allow them to learn a little about your business and introduce them to your brand. They will know what to expect from your profile when they read your bio. The limit on characters for a Twitter bio is 160, so you need to think before you fill it in. You need to write a bio that represents your brand successfully and reflects your brand value.

Use Images and Videos

Use images and videos in your content whenever possible, as it makes your tweets more visually appealing to viewers. Statistics show that tweets containing images tend to outperform those that are purely text. You can add an engaging and eye-catching element to your tweets by adding a photo or image. This will make users on Twitter take note of your tweet when it appears on their feed. In fact, tweets with videos outperform those with images as well. You can get more than six times the usual engagement that your tweets usually get if you use videos. You can create videos to show how your products are created or used. You can use images to show your products in an attractive way. These are the ways in which you can increase engagement on your tweets.

Share Media Mentions

When you see your business being mentioned in any media, you should share that article, image, or video on your tweets. It helps establish more legitimacy for your business. A user who sees your business in the media will be more likely to trust the authenticity of your brand. It will also show them that a lot of people are aware of your brand and enjoying the products or services you offer. Sharing media mentions is a great way to broadcast brand success to any audience. You can use this to add backlinks to the source of the media mention. This will drive traffic to that media website and boost their following as well. If you benefit their business, that media outlet is also more likely to mention your business more often.

Promote Events

An effective way to promote your business events is to use Twitter for it. You can create hashtags for any event you are holding and schedule some tweets to promote it. It could be anything from a launch party to any other content. Followers will be informed about your event and can find a way to participate, attend, or sign up for the event. Promoting the event will help you reach followers and other Twitter users as well.

Keep Checking Your Direct Messages

Twitter has a feature called Direct Message inbox where users can contact you directly in a private message. They can use this feature to send you any queries, comments, or concerns they may have. You need to check the inbox regularly to ensure that you are providing optimal customer service. You should respond and engage with these users as often as possible. It will contribute to what people think of your business in the long run.

Keep Tracking Analytics

You have probably been putting in a lot of effort into your Twitter marketing campaign. At some point, you have to check if your efforts are paying off. You need to check if you are closer to meeting your goals and if your strategy is helping you get more followers, leads, and conversions. Analyzing your work will help you determine your success on Twitter.

Track the following metrics on Twitter:

- Engagement

- Impressions

- Hashtags

- Top tweets

- Contributors

Twitter will be a powerful social media marketing tool for your business, and you need to start taking advantage of it. Consider using Twitter for business tactics and make use of the various marketing tactics that have been mentioned in the text above. Sign up and start tweeting today!

Chapter Eight

LinkedIn Marketing 101

L inkedIn has usually been at the forefront and a pioneer in the world of professional online networking and professional social networking, making it a household name in most cities.

However, LinkedIn becomes a mere afterthought when people are looking for different social media marketing strategies to boost their pages or online businesses. Overlooking LinkedIn as a potential social media marketing tool is a mistake that you do not want to make.

LinkedIn is one of the most powerful "business-to-business" or B2B tools that are available in today's online ecosystem that can help you create a buzz around your businesses and thereby boost your revenue. By employing the right marketing strategies, LinkedIn can turn out to be immensely useful in shaping your business model and building your brand.

- In order to generate fruitful leads, you must learn how to identify and target the right B2B audience. Learning how to do this will also help you to save time and resources.

- To establish and solidify your brand, learn how to strategically create content that will help establish your business as the best in your niche or industry.

- Track and measure your performance. This will help you understand if your strategies are working or if you need to make any adjustments.

With the application of all these basic principles, you will be able to successfully build the perfect LinkedIn online marketing strategy that will help your business become successful.

Determine Your Goals

As is the case with any business model, the first step of the process involves goal development and figuring out what the short term and long-term goals of your company are. In most types of online marketing strategies, the primary goals are:

- To generate more leads.

- To drive more Internet traffic to your website.

- To increase online impressions or content shares.

- To establish your brand as an expert or as the best in the particular field that you are involved in.

After you have established your goals and everything else set in place, you can start to look for ways in which LinkedIn can contribute towards achieving these goals.

Some of the most common benefits of using LinkedIn as a media marketing tool are:

Lead Generation

LinkedIn has one of the highest conversion rates when it comes to social media and networking platforms. According to a survey done by HubSpot, LinkedIn visitors tend to convert to leads 277% more often than visitors that are present on other networking or social media platforms.

Recruitment

LinkedIn and other social, professional networking platforms happen to be the number one source of quality recruits and hires. These platforms tend to fetch more well-rounded individuals compared to common job portals of recruitment agencies.

Brand Awareness

LinkedIn is a professional networking platform that has been built for the very sole purpose of creating a network of connections. This feature of LinkedIn can help you kickstart and improve brand awareness as it allows you to connect with your potential audience or leads directly.

Establishing Authority

Unlike most networking platforms or social media sites, LinkedIn has a more professional base. This allows you to share information with potential audiences directly, and if done in the right way, it can help your business establish authority in the particular niche that it belongs to. The effectiveness of this depends on the content you create, and we shall look into this later.

How LinkedIn can help boost your business and fetch better leads can depend on the type of goals that have been set by you and your business development team. For instance, if one of your primary business goals is to increase the number of leads generated by your company by 50% or more, the ease of networking and information exchange that LinkedIn provides can help you reach these overarching business goals.

Tracking Conversions from LinkedIn Using Google Analytics

In order to set your lead generation goals, the first and most important step is identifying a proper baseline. To do that, open your Google Analytics tool, find and select the option "Acquisition," and then enter the "Social" sub-menu. Once you have entered "Social," select the "Conversions" option and then click on "LinkedIn." Once you have entered this section, you will have to set your dates back and gather conversion data from the last six months.

To be able to track that data, you will need to have goals set for whenever your lead conversion occurs. That brings us to lead conversions. What exactly is lead generation? If a potential customer or visitor fills out a "Contact Us" form that will usually be present on your LinkedIn page, this generates a lead. The total number of lead conversions that you get will be your baseline, and it will also help you determine and track growth percentages or any decline in lead conversions. For instance, let's say that your business has converted a total of 1000 leads in the past six months, and now you want to increase the lead conversion rate by 25%. This means that you will have to add 250 more leads in the coming six months in order to achieve your target. In addition, LinkedIn has come out with LinkedIn Lead Gen Forms, an online form that is an easy method to collect information from your profile.

Establishing Your Business as the Expert in Your Industry Using LinkedIn

How can you establish your business as the expert or the best in the field that it is involved in? How can you build a strong and dependable reputation? Can you do it by publishing more content, or can you do it by being more hands-on, jumping in, and interacting with LinkedIn groups more often.

If you think that sharing more content and posting more often in different WhatsApp groups will automatically establish and boost your authority, you are in for a rude awakening. Establishing your authority is not just about posting more content. You need to make sure that whatever you are sharing needs to be engaging, informative, thought-provoking, and authentic. Although there are such specific metrics or indicators that are can specifically tell you about the authority of your business, you can still make roughly accurate inferences by tracking metrics like an increase in followers, numbers of shares, and relevant engagement that your content is garnering.

You must be wondering, "Why those specific metrics only?" The answer is fairly simple. If you have a greater number of followers, your content will begin receiving more shares and create better online "impressions." This also means that a larger part of your audience will actually interact with your posts. This inherently means that your audience is finding value in the content that you are producing.

Tracking and Creating Goals around These Metrics

Follower growth, shares, and quality of engagement are metrics that can easily be found using in-app analytics. In order to do that, go to your LinkedIn page and click on the "Followers" option in the drop-down menu to check your follower growth and you can also click on the "Updates" option in the same drop-down menu to find the growth of shares and other overall message interactions.

To set a proper baseline, you can either factor in the average growth that has been recorded for the past six months of your posts/content, or you can also take the average growth that has been recorded for the week and determine a proper baseline for your goals according to the average value that you get. Your team will be assisting you throughout this process, so make sure that you put enough effort into figuring out what your team wants and how much do they want to grow that baseline.

Find the Right Audience

You will never be able to create great content if you do not know whom you are creating it for or who/what you're targeting it towards. The next step of your LinkedIn marketing strategy will be figuring out who your potential target audiences are. Without doing this, your marketing strategies will likely turn out to be unsuccessful, so make sure that you don't overlook this step.

LinkedIn is a business-to-business (B2B) networking channel. You cannot merely transfer your content from other social media sites such as Facebook or Instagram and expect it to be accepted as good content. The audience types that are predominantly active on LinkedIn have different needs, and these needs have to be catered in a very specific way.

While identifying your target audiences, you will need to consider these factors:

- Who are your target audiences?

- What type of problems or difficulties are they facing?

- In what areas of business are they experiencing these problems?

- When are they experiencing these problems?

- Why are they experiencing these problems?

Optimizing Your LinkedIn Profile for Maximum Exposure

One of the final steps in your LinkedIn marketing strategy will be optimizing your LinkedIn profile for having maximum exposure to your target audiences.

Set Your Profile Picture

Your LinkedIn profile picture should clearly display your company logo, so make sure that the image you use meets the optimum size requirements that LinkedIn offers. The recommended resolution of LinkedIn profile pictures is 400×400 pixels.

Utilize Your Banner

Your LinkedIn page will look more engaging and possess more personality if you use the right image for your LinkedIn page banner. You can make use of standard CTA or call-to-action buttons, or you can choose something that's more unique and makes your page stand out, such as a good quality photo of your office premises.

Complete Your Bio

The "Bio" or biography section happens to be one of the most overlooked parts of any social profile, regardless of the type of social media platform you are using. Although this may seem like a small and irrelevant detail to deal with or account for in your marketing strategies, having an incomplete or blank "Bio" will cause you to miss out on various opportunities of interacting with your customer base and target audiences.

The best thing about the LinkedIn bio section is that it is very easy to edit with features such as drag and drop that allow you to incorporate different pieces of content from your website directly. Your LinkedIn "bio" should include the following:

An Informative Company Overview

The person with the most knowledge about your company will be you; you know better than anyone else what your company stands for and what it is all about. Use your bio to tell your audiences what you and your company stand for and what you are all about. If you have a mission statement or a motto that your business organization lives by, then you can add them in to provide more character to your LinkedIn bio.

Information about the Products or Services That You Offer

If you want your business to pick up and do well, you will need to do something that is setting you apart from the rest of the crowd when it comes to the niche that you are involved in. If one of your potential leads is experiencing problems, how can your company be the best choice for them when it comes to finding solutions to these problems? If your target audiences or potential do not know what type of services to offer, it is less likely for them to choose you over your competitors.

Peer Recommendations

Most people trust the recommendation of peers and other customers over any type of self-advertising campaign. Showcasing any stellar recommendations that you receive from any existing clients or customers can improve the chances of gaining new customers. If someone is still on the fence about choosing to employ the services of your company, the best way to persuade them is by showcasing good customer and client reviews or recommendations.

Establishing Voice and Tone

The next part of your strategy will involve creating a professional voice and tone for your LinkedIn page. According to Buffer.com, your voice is your brand personality described in a few adjectives, while your tone will add a specific flavor to your voice, which depends on several other factors or situations.

Let's get started by establishing your voice. To do that, try to define your brand personality clearly. Is the general image of your brand informative, purposeful, political, or thoughtful? You can always take help from your team while developing your LinkedIn profile and bio. Start by getting them to write down three adjectives that best describe your brand voice. You can determine the final three that your company LinkedIn bio is going to embody by taking a common vote that includes every person in your team.

Once you have determined your keywords and adjectives, you can begin to decide how your voice sounds like on LinkedIn. Your voice should be outright confrontational or overly aggressive, and it also should not be overly modest; finding that balance between being professional and personal is what works best for most LinkedIn pages.

Chapter Nine

Pinterest Marketing 101

A lot of people think that Facebook or Twitter are the only platforms useful for social media marketing. If you are one of them, you need to rethink this notion. Pinterest is one social media platform that you need to take seriously. A Pinterest pin is a lot more spreadable than a tweet that might go viral. On average, retweets are only done at a 1.4% rate. The half-life of a post on Facebook is much lesser than that of a pin. Pinterest has become one of the most popular platforms for business marketing of late. Pinterest actually has more than 200 million users, and the user database is growing every day. Last year, there was a large increase in the number of accounts created by Fortune 500 companies. There are hundreds of thousands of businesses already on Pinterest, and we think you should be one too. Pinterest is not just about checking out pictures of exotic locations or DIY projects. It has a lot of integrated features that are ideal for businesses.

A Pinterest account for business is different from a Pinterest account for personal use

Having a business account on Pinterest has its own perks. Having a personal account will not work as well as the Pinterest for a Business account, so you need to sign up for that if you haven't already. It will help you to tap into the full potential of marketing on Pinterest. The following are some of the perks of a business account:

- Terms of Service for Business accounts are different from personal accounts. One reason for this is that the account will be used for commercial purposes. The Acceptable Use Policy, as well as the Pin Etiquette Policy, will remain the same. They just add a few guidelines to be followed when you are using the Pinterest account for commercial purposes. Firstly, you should not be promoting spam by doing things like asking people to comment multiple times. You should also not run contests where you ask people to repin and count multiple repins as entries in the content. It is discouraged to run any such contests, promotions or sweepstakes too often. You should also not suggest to users that your business is sponsored or endorsed by Pinterest.

- Pinterest provides educational marketing material. While you use Pinterest as a platform for marketing your business, they also provide you with materials to learn how you can effectively carry it out. You can use the Pinterest Blog for now to learn a lot, but they are also working on launching webinars, workshops, and resources that will be useful for small businesses in particular.

- Pinterest Analytics is available. One of the newer features of a Pinterest business account is the Pinterest Analytics tool. After verifying your business account, you will be allowed to access a lot of tracking information. It will help you monitor the performance of your content and overall strategy. This will help you constantly modify and improve your marketing campaign.

- Five types of Rich Pins. Pinterest gives you Rich Pins of five different types, and each of these has more information than the usual pins. This is why they have serious sales power. These Rich Pins include information like real-time price or stock updates, map locations, and even direct links to your business website.

- New tools to be launched. Pinterest is working on introducing some more new tools for business account users. Staying updated with their newsletter will keep you updated on any new promotions or announcements. Some of such tools include Promoted Pins and Widget Builder.

- Settings are different. For a personal account, you have to use the formula of First name and Last name. Business account users are allowed to use their business name itself. The account will also not have any automatic link to your personal Facebook account. You will have to add a tab for Facebook if you want to direct users to your profile.

Create Popular Pins

If you execute your pins the right way, you can get a lot of engagement on your account. Social Media Examiner has described Pinterest as a visual search engine. Like a blog article or Instagram account, you will want your content on Pinterest to be searchable as well. Your pins won't be seen if you don't make them searchable. This is why it is important to understand the Pinterest culture first by studying what your audience is searching for. You have to learn how to create a popular pin before you start pinning from your business account.

Popular Categories

Learning about popular Pinterest categories will help you understand what boards will help you with your business. According to statistics, 80% of the users on Pinterest are females, and the rest are males. However, the last year has seen an increase in male users by nearly two times. You have to figure out what board is relevant for your business. You can't post pins about DIY crafts if your business is related to something completely different. Some of the popular pin categories preferred by females are food, drinks, DIY, home decor, and fashion. For males, the popular categories include health, fitness, products, animals, and celebrities.

Images that Work

Anyone who uses Pinterest knows that it is a very visual site. Even if you open the site for the very first time, the visual aspect becomes very obvious. The images that you pin on Pinterest will be the cornerstone for your pins due to this. For a popular Pinterest pin, your images should be high resolution and clear. It has also been noticed that people prefer lighter images as compared to darker ones and repin those more often. An image without a face is also more likely to get a repin.

Optimal Pin Size

Any pin on Pinterest will have equal width, but the length is unlimited. For a typical pin, 736x1102 pixels are ideal. This size of the pin is neither too large nor too small. Since the template on Pinterest is of that size, it makes it easier for you to create the right size of pins.

Instructographics

At times you need to consider making use of the longer length allowed for pins. Instructographic is just a Pinterest name for infographic.

They are popular because of the how-to nature of their content. DIYs are a very popular category on Pinterest.

Optimizing Pins and Getting Them Seen or Shared

Creating a great pin is just the first step. The main work is to get this pin seen and shared by more people. If the pin is not optimized, no one will be able to find the pin.

Best Time to Pin

You can figure out the best time to post, depending on the habits of your target audience. You should test and check what the best time is for pinning. According to HubSpot, the best time for a business to post is a Saturday morning. On normal days, you should post between 2 P.M. - 4 P.M. or 8 P.M. - 1 A.M.

Content From Your Sites Should be Easy to Pin

If you post on any sites, add a Pin It button over the image. WordPress allows you to add a plugin for the Pinterest Pin It Hover button. This kind of simple to integrate buttons will direct visitors from your site to your Pinterest account. It will also help them pin your content on their own Pinterest accounts if they want. If you don't use such buttons, it won't bring any interaction from your site to Pinterest.

Connect to Other Social Media Accounts

Connect your Pinterest account to other social media accounts for your business. Getting more followers is a task in itself on any new social media account. This is why you need to utilize the following that you already have on other social media accounts. Let people on those accounts know of your presence on Pinterest and ask them to support you on that platform as well. It is easy to connect the Pinterest business account to Twitter or Facebook. Tapping into the following you already have will help you get a real head start. You can also use Pinterest to get new followers on those other accounts by adding buttons on the account. The account settings on Pinterest will allow you to connect your Twitter and Facebook accounts quite easily. However, you can only connect a personal Facebook account and not a page.

Use Your Newsletter to Share Pins

Instead of waiting for people to find your pins, make it easier for them to find the pins. One easy way to do this is by adding your latest pins on your newsletter. This will direct your subscribers to your Pinterest account when they receive the newsletter and if they are interested in those pins.

SEO

SEO is important for social media marketing, and this applies to Pinterest as well. An efficient SEO strategy is important in order to get discovered by people. Thankfully, it is not very difficult to optimize pins for a Pinterest search. Do research for the keywords related to your pins and business. You can use tools like the Google AdWords Keyword Planner for this. It will help you find a lot of relevant keywords to use for your pins. Your pin title should include these keywords to optimize search. The pin description should also include keywords. Add keywords to the pin image file names as well. Remember not to use too many keywords, even while using SEO. Using too many keywords in the same title or description will be too much. Instead, find a way to use a good keyword for the right context.

Call-to-Pin

You know how call-to-actions work for ad copy. Similarly, you need to use a call-to-pin for your pins in order to increase engagement. It will help you get about 80% more engagement than you would without a CTP. Add a simple CTP in the pin description when you create a post.

Build Relationships with Viewers and Gain More Followers by Increasing Engagement

You now know enough about popular pins and getting more views on your pins. The next step is using these pins to build relationships with your target audience. This includes followers as well as influencers to help grow your brand reach. The more reach you get, the more success it will result in. You have to know what your audience usually looks for when they are following other business accounts. This will help you understand what kind of content you should be providing for them as well. A study showed that Pinterest users take note of a few factors when they are deciding if they should follow a new business account or not. One factor is how many followers that account has and how many accounts they are following. Another factor is the number of pins that account has. They also take note of the number of boards they have.

You need to use the following tips to stay on top of these factors and also to build relationships with more viewers:

Post More Frequently

You can pin more frequently on Pinterest as compared to other social media sites. Having 5-30 pins every day will help you get a lot more followers on Pinterest. You can repin others content but focus on pinning your own content. Even though you can pin multiple pins in a day, don't do it within a short span of time. Post after a while, and spread your pins throughout the day. You can also create a secret board and keep pins collected there to help save time. Every morning or even every week, load up on pins on that board and then return to that board so you can use the pins on a live board.

Engage with Followers

Followers may leave questions or comments on your pins. Engage with them by responding to these comments. Addressing people directly will help you take your customer service to an even higher level and make followers appreciate the engagement. Ignoring comments frequently will result in an unfollow.

Pay Attention to Pins from Followers

If you want engagement on your content, you should return the favor as well. Check your follower's boards and leave some comments on their pins. They will love the attention, and it will build a positive image around your business. It is also an easy way to get noticed by their followers.

Engage with Popular Accounts

Follow popular brands and engage with them. These are the accounts that you can learn a lot from. Take note of the kind of content they post and what kind of boards they have. You should also take note of their engagement rate so you can get on that level as well. When you comment on pins that are popular, it will attract attention from people who follow those pins. This will direct traffic to your account and help you gain followers. Follow popular boards that are relevant to the industry you are in. Don't follow random accounts just because they are popular. If the account category has nothing to do with your business, it won't help you to engage with them either. You have to connect with users who are connected to your industry, so engage with such accounts.

Invite Other Users to Pin on Your Boards

The Open Board is a cool feature that allows users to contribute pins to other boards. You can give users this access to your board by adding their email or name. The creator of the board has veto power over the board, and none of these users will be able to change the description or name of the board. This feature is an advantage for marketers because it helps get the community more involved. You can invite followers to pin on your Open Board. It is even better if other leaders in your industry contribute pins to your board.

Build Relationships with Influencers

There are a lot of Influencers in each field, and you can leverage the reach of the influencers in your field to help grow your account. Reach out to influencers by following their board and repining their pins. Leave comments on the pins they post and engage with them. You can initiate a collaboration with influencers in this way. You can ask them to contribute to your board or even do the same for them. You can show them that you are an expert in your field and give them ideas for their board. Acting professional will help you get interested in the influencer as well.

Find Friends From Other Accounts

When you sign up on any social media account like Instagram, they ask you to find friends from contacts or your Facebook friends list. You also have this option for Pinterest, so utilize it to get a foundation of followers on the account. You can follow these friends on Pinterest and let them know of your presence. They will probably follow you back as well since you already have a relationship with them on other social media.

Pinterest Strategies to promote your business successfully.

Promote your Brand

Integrate Rich Pins

Rich Pins are given this name for a reason. When a brand uses Rich Pins, they tend to see a huge jump in their ration of repins and pins. If you take a look at popular brands like Target, you will see how they take advantage of these Rich Pins. It doesn't mean that you will be rolling in a pile of money just because you use some Rich Pins. However, these Rich Pins are a valuable asset on Pinterest and will give you a lot of valuable information to generate traffic. Growing sales on Pinterest is made much easier by using these. The five types of Rich Pins are recipe, movie, article, place, and product. All of these are full of their own valuable features that help to boost engagement and direct traffic.

Advantages of using Rich Pins

On applying for Rich Pins, you will be getting real-time information on your pins automatically. You will also find it easier to direct more people to your website since Rich Pins are linked to the site. This is a no-fuss way to get more leads. Article pins are useful because they help in promoting blog posts, and you can then direct followers from Pinterest to your blog. These come with a large title that includes the brand logo and also includes a description with a call to action linked to the website.

How to Integrate a Rich Pin

In order to direct traffic to your website using Rich Pins, the pins have to be validated on Pinterest first. If you are not a tech-savvy person, you need to get someone on your team to do it. It involves the use of Meta tags in a few simple steps. Once Pinterest approves your Rich Pins, everyone on Pinterest can easily view them. They will directly be taken to your site with these approved Rich Pins. Using Rich Pins is not just a suggestion; you absolutely have to utilize these for success on Pinterest. Since this feature is fairly new, you can be among the businesses that are taking advantage of it at the right stage. It will help you stand apart from a lot of others who are using Rich Pins. Follow the examples of the big brands that are successfully integrating Rich Pins as a part of their Pinterest marketing strategy.

Mix Up Your Content

On any social media account, you need to mix up the content appropriately. If not, you will easily lose interest from your followers. It will also affect your chances of gaining any new ones in the future, and this will affect your growth rate negatively. Posting product photos is not enough, even if your goal is to drive sales. The diversity of your pins is an important factor that determines if people will follow your account. Give your followers more value by adding diverse boards and to prevent a monotonous feed.

Include Direct Links to Your Website

Every pin does not have to be a Rich Pin. There are certain kinds of content that will not benefit from the information that is provided by a Rich Pin. This is why you have to pay attention to the context and decide if it should just be a regular pin. In your brand inspiration board, you don't necessarily have to use Rich Pins. Just post relevant pins on the board. However, you do need to add a direct link to the main business website on these regular pins. Rich Pins are directly linked to your site, but here you have to add the link yourself. No matter what your pin is about, just add a link in the description section of the pin so that viewers can visit your site. You never know when a simple pin catches the fancy of a viewer, and they may want to check your brand out even more. Adding a link to the site ensures that they can do this in an easy manner.

The Popular Boards Should be Put on Top

As you keep up with activity on Pinterest, you will be able to make out how popular each of your boards are. The boards that get more engagement should be moved to the top of your page. When any new visitor comes to your page, they should be able to view the best material you have put forward on Pinterest. New viewers will usually follow your account based on the first impression they get from your page.

Content Should be Relevant and Seasonal

It is important to keep your content fresh. You can use the changes in seasons, holidays, or any special events to create a theme for your content. Adding relevancy will catch more attention from viewers. It will also make your products and services more appealing to customers at the time.

A Blog Posts Board

Keep a separate board just for the Rich Pins from your account. Keep this particular board at the top of your page, among other boards. Followers should be able to see this as the first board when they visit your page. It will draw more traffic to the main site and also make it easier for users to find any content you post. Followers will appreciate the fact that you put this content together on a board that makes it easier for them to find it.

Utilize Pinterest Analytics to track success and differentiate between successful and non-successful strategies

The Pinterest Analytics tool is one of the most helpful features introduced by them. It is only available for business accounts, and you can make use of it for your marketing efforts.

It allows the user to see the following information:

- Which pins or boards you post are popular among your viewers

- Which pins from your site have people saved?

- Who your audience is on Pinterest?

- What devices people use when people view your content

- How the Pin It button generates traffic to your website

You may wonder why these statistics are important for you. It is because they are important for optimizing your account and helping your reach grow. Information gathered from Pinterest analytics will help you understand which strategies are working for your brand and which you need to modify. This information will also help you build a better Pinterest strategy for future use. However, you have to get your website verified in order to get access to the Pinterest analytics feature. We also recommend that you get your website verified for another reason; it helps gain trust and build authority. The red checkmark for your website shows users on Pinterest that your business is legit. In the settings section, you can add a Meta tag and get your website verified. You may choose not to get the website verified and still add a link to it, but you will be denied access to Pinterest analytics in this case.

Don't feel overwhelmed with the amount of information that we have thrown your way. Once you start putting this information to use, you will see how easy it is to use Pinterest for a successful marketing campaign. So, get started and get pinning.

Chapter Ten

Mistakes to Avoid in Social Media Marketing

Considering the number of people actively using social media on a daily basis, social media marketing is a no-brainer choice for any business looking for greater exposure. While it is fairly simple to be successful in a social media campaign, you can also make mistakes that work against you. There are many businesses that barely manage to run a good marketing campaign on social media. There are a lot of things you may be doing right, but there are also just as many that you might be doing wrong.

The following are some of the common mistakes that marketers make in social media marketing that you need to look out for:

- Not having a plan.

- Treating every social media platform in the same way.

- Assuming that everyone is your audience.

- Buying followers.

- Using the wrong tone.

- Having more accounts than you can manage.

- Using too many irrelevant hashtags.

- Not replying to comments.

- Lacking a social media policy.

- Deleting any negative comments left by viewers.

- Having an uninteresting campaign.

Not Having a Plan

Many people get started with social media marketing without actually putting together a strategy for their campaign. The first step should always be to take time and understand the possibilities of using social media for your business. A guide can only help you take steps. If you follow the steps without understanding your audience or without knowledge of marketing, you won't know the direction in which the campaign will go. The lack of a plan can make all your efforts go to waste. Set goals, create a budget, and plan of action that you can follow. You should figure out what you want to accomplish and also how you plan to do it. Set parameters to measure results as well.

Treating Every Social Media Platform in the Same Way

The audience on each social media platform is looking for something unique to that particular platform. You cannot treat every platform in the same way. If your content or campaign is inconsistent with the flow of that network, your effort will be counterproductive. There are little details that you have to notice and customize as you keep the audience in mind. For instance, when you are creating an ad for different regions, you have to keep the languages of those places in mind as well. You cannot run an ad in Spanish in a place where people don't speak Spanish. If you want your social media marketing to be effective across each platform, you have to customize it and keep the differences between these platforms in mind. Communicate with the audience in the manner of that particular platform.

Assuming That Everyone is Your Audience

Social media is used by a lot of people, but not everyone is your target audience. You have to understand and work around this. To create an effective social media plan, it is integral to know who your audience is. The oversimplification of an audience will distort the ability of that business to understand their audience. For instance, you cannot make a generalization that all millennials are your audience because they really are not. Millennials are a whole generation, and everyone has their own needs and interests and wants. You have to figure out the demographics of people who will really be interested in what your brand offers. You need to have more precise targeting for effective marketing. Understanding your audience will also set a tone for how you deal with them and what kind of content you create.

Buying Followers

It is a well-known fact that buying followers are against the guidelines of social media in general. However, it is tempting for anyone starting out with social media marketing. When you see that the number of your followers is growing at a very slow rate, you may want to pay for a sudden surge in the number. However, when you do this, you may, in fact, be paying for problems. Facebook and Instagram have an algorithm, and buying followers goes against it. The algorithm thinks it is a good post when you get a lot of likes and comments. However, when you pay for followers, these accounts don't engage in any activity. They are simply fake accounts that add a number to your follower count. This means that your engagement rate is contradictory to your follower count. The fake follows and likes to tend to harm business. This pushes the platforms to delete such spam accounts. When you pay for fake followers, it will cause your posts to appear even less on the feeds of the real followers you have. This is why you need to skip this seemingly easy way to grow your brand and do it organically.

Using the Wrong Tone

On social media, you have the freedom to say or do what you want. This is applicable to personal accounts because you are just sharing with friends or family. However, a business account cannot be as careless in their actions on social media. The behavior of a brand on any social media account is subject to a lot of scrutinizes. Your brand voice has to be interesting and also friendly towards your audience. You cannot be too official, nor can you be too casual. Find the right tone to connect with the audience. Don't try using jokes that may be offensive to a certain group of people, either. You have to stop and reflect on the tone of any post you make on any social media platform. Your tone will reflect your brand and affect how the audience perceives you.

Having More Accounts Than You Can Manage

A lot of businesses jump on every single social network platform that they can. This is not a mistake that you want to repeat. Setting up all these accounts would mean that you have that many accounts to manage. Don't stretch your resources thin by taking on more than you can handle. This kind of tactic can actually cause you to miss out on seeing any results from social media marketing. One person cannot usually handle more than 2-3 social media accounts in an effective way. So, don't assign any marketer more than this workload if you want them to work well. If you have a big marketing team, you can afford to distribute the workload among them and have a larger social media presence. However, when the person to handle it is less, stick to the main big platforms like Facebook and Twitter. Prioritize efforts on the platform that produces more results for the business.

Using too many Irrelevant Hashtags

Hashtags are an easy way to help people search for your content. However, you should not overuse hashtags and add endless hashtags to your post when they are irrelevant to your content. A lot of people add tons of popular hashtags to their posts even when those tags are not related to their posts. This can be very annoying for an audience looking for something in particular. You also have to be careful about using hashtags that might be offensive to people. Don't capitalize on the wrong things just to grab more attention for your content. Stick to hashtags that are basic, relevant, or specific to your brand. Don't do something that will make people question the values of your brand.

Not Replying to Comments

As we have already mentioned many times in the book, engagement rates are important. You can boost engagement rates a lot by having more comments on your posts. This is especially important for platforms like Facebook and Instagram. Not only do a higher number of comments appeal to the algorithm, but they also appeal to customers, and that is more important. When customers leave comments on your posts, they appreciate being replied to or even just some attention by receiving alike on the comment. Being silent on social media will be a major mistake and create a negative impression on your audience. If you don't respond to comments, people are less likely to engage in your content in the future.

Lacking a Social Media Policy

If your business does not have a specified social media policy, it can cause a lot of problems and even result in public embarrassment for your company. Your various social media accounts may be managed by different people, but there should be a general policy for everyone to follow. There has to be a guideline for what is considered acceptable and what is not. Content that is racist, sexist, offensive, derogatory, obscene, religious, or discriminatory is usually considered off-limits for most businesses. You don't want to offend any potential customers on social media. Making one such mistake can cause viral defamation of your company. This is why you have to create a good social media policy that everyone in your company adheres to. The policy has to cover creation as well as the management of social media accounts. Restrict access to the various accounts to prevent any untrustworthy person from accessing it. A single mistake on social media can turn into a PR nightmare for your company.

Deleting any Negative Comments Left by Viewers

There are times when a customer might be dissatisfied with your product, service, or just some content you posted. They may leave a long, ugly comment on your post or timeline due to this. This is something you might have noticed many brands do, but it is a mistake you should not repeat. It shows inauthenticity. Show people that you are not afraid of criticism and that your brand takes any complaints seriously. Responding to negative comments with a positive tone will only reflect positively on your brand. Thank such people for bringing any issues to your notice and let them know that you will work to solve it. When it comes to some people who leave toxic comments, it is best just to ignore them. However, if it is toxic and directed at someone, in particular, you can choose to block such users.

Having an Uninteresting Campaign

Social media has millions of posts on a daily basis. If you create content that is boring or uninteresting, your post will be lost among the masses. You have to strive to create something that instantly grabs the attention of your target audience. You can't just post random pictures of products and expect people to buy it. You have to research your audience and create content that they would love to see. Take inspiration from other accounts that are successfully running social media marketing campaigns and do it better for your own.

Relying Heavily on Automation

Automation makes your work very easy while managing social media campaigns. However, you cannot rely solely on automated posting on these accounts. Social media is about interaction. It is not just about setting up some automated posts for the audience to see. If you don't interact or if everything is too automated, your audience will feel detached from your business. Lacking a personal touch will work against your business. Don't set up automated replies to messages or comments, either. People notice such small details and appreciate it when they are given personal attention. Impersonal exchanges will make customers distance themselves and drift towards other brands that pay more attention. Posting too much automatic content that is irrelevant will also make them want to unfollow you. Find ways in which your audience will feel more connected with your brand and appreciate the content of your post.

Social media principles to keep in mind:

- Only use social media platforms that make sense for your brand or business

- Evaluate everything to make sure that your efforts are giving you results

- Always post at the right time to reach your target audience

- Build connections by interacting with your audience

- Make use of visual media and don't throw blocks of boring data at your audience

- Make your presence on each social media platform unique

- Share content that is useful for your viewers so that they appreciate your brand

- Strike a good balance between professionalism and friendliness for your audience

- Don't keep selling even if it is your main objective

- Always re-check your content before posting

If you keep these simple principles in mind, your social media marketing campaign will be successful.

Conclusion

Social media platforms have taken the world by storm in the last decade or so, and it is ever-growing. It is essential for every business to utilize the benefits of social media to help their brand grow.

The social media strategies mentioned in this book are easy to apply and will definitely show results if you execute them well. So, start creating a profile for your business on any of the platforms mentioned in the book and start marketing!

References

https://www.hubspot.com/Facebook-marketing

https://www.wordstream.com/blog/ws/2013/04/15/Facebook-marketing

https://neilpatel.com/blog/Facebook-marketing/

https://www.bluefountainmedia.com/blog/advantages-of-social-media-marketing

https://coschedule.com/blog/benefits-of-social-media-marketing-for-business/

https://neilpatel.com/what-is-social-media-marketing/

https://www.wordstream.com/blog/ws/2019/12/11/social-media-marketing-mistakes

https://www.intechnic.com/blog/10-common-social-media-marketing-mistakes-to-avoid/

https://www.wordstream.com/blog/ws/2015/01/06/instagram-marketing

https://neilpatel.com/blog/ultimate-Pinterest-marketing-guide/

https://coschedule.com/blog/LinkedIn-marketing-strategy/